KEEPING IT SIMPLE

YASMIN FAHR

KEEPING IT SIMPLE

EASY WEEKNIGHT 🍲 ONE-POT RECIPES

Hardie Grant

BOOKS

BRIGHT DISHES FOR COLD DAYS 63

GLUTEN, GRAINS AND GOOD STUFF 85

SALAD FOR DINNER 119

LOOK MORE IMPRESSIVE THAN THEY ARE 143

INTRODUCTION

When I was 11 years old, I woke up early on the morning of my younger sister Ashley's birthday to make her banana pancakes. I remember sneaking out of my room in the still-quiet house, trying to keep our dog from getting hyper and waking everyone up as she followed me into the kitchen. She sat, watching me, as I whisked the batter, cut the bananas, got out the orange juice and set the table.

Oh man... the pancakes were awful. I dropped one on the floor and our dog, who would gobble up anything, sniffed it and walked away. It was not a great start to my culinary career.

Despite that blip, food and cooking are an integral part of my life, whether it's learning about different cultures through food, visiting markets around the world or having friends over for dinner. And while I love dining out in restaurants more than anything, taking that little bit of time to cook for myself, a loved one or a few, is a form of self-care. Slowing it down is a way to ground myself, spend quality time with people I love and feed myself something delicious that's also good for me.

The point of this book is to encourage you to cook more at home and enjoy the process. You'll find reliable recipes for weeknight dinners, easy and approachable cooking techniques for roasting a chicken, cooking a whole fish, searing scallops and lots of kitchen shortcuts. Soon you'll start to learn things without even realising it and, in turn, will become a better cook. My goal is that you'll have dinner on the table in the time that it takes you to drink a glass of wine. Maybe two. These recipes are for all of us who love food, want to feel good, find ourselves short on time and don't want to end up with a kitchen full of dirty dishes.

The best part? All of these recipes can be made in one pot or pan (sometimes with another thrown in for prep), don't require a lot of skill – but taste like they do – and tend to be on the lighter side. That's not in terms of substance, as they are well-portioned, filling main courses, but more in terms of making sure they are healthy(ish).

So, now that you know what you're getting yourself into, my definition of 'healthy' for these recipes loosely means that there will be no butter (maybe some ghee), very little dairy (other than feta, mozzarella and Parmesan, because I love them, and really, who doesn't?) and more lean than fatty meats. You'll also probably catch me sneaking something green into everything I can.

As we all know, but maybe don't put into practice enough, being healthy is not just what you eat, but how you live your life, from how much you sleep and how much exercise you do, to thinking positively and incorporating care for yourself and others into your daily actions and thoughts. You're superhuman and my hero if you don't feel anxiety in this social media-infused, tech-loaded era, which is why I think those last few things are so important now more than ever. And that's how I define being healthy: feeling good in your body and day-to-day to life.

My goal is to empower you to feel confident in the kitchen, as I know how intimidating and overwhelming it can feel until you get the hang of it. I think you'll find that there's something deeply satisfying about the ability to feed yourself and the people you care about with food that is both beautiful and nourishing. And, hopefully, the stories and tales sprinkled throughout will make it feel like I'm in the kitchen with you, guiding you along over a glass of wine.

HOW TO USE THIS BOOK

Most of us, myself included, are not aspiring to be the next MasterChef (at least not admittedly), so the recipes in this book are meant to help you become a better home cook. I aim to do this by providing you with tips and tricks that I've learned from fellow cookbook authors and talented chefs who were kind enough to bestow some of their knowledge onto me.

For example, there's a list of commonly used words and phrases that took me a while to figure out (like the difference between a gentle and active simmer), efficiency recommendations so you can maximise your time in the kitchen, plus ways to use leftovers and leftover ingredients so nothing rots in your fridge and goes to waste.

Follow the recipes, pay attention to what you like and don't like, and soon, you'll be tweaking them and adapting them to your personal preferences; we all tend to have different peculiarities (you'll get a sense of mine, soon enough). Yes, you might mess something up (you can blame me), but hopefully you'll learn from it and get it right next time. The best thing about cooking is that there is always a next time.

Where to start
All of the recipes are simple and don't require a lot of skill, so you can bounce around the chapters or start anywhere you'd like and have some fun with it. In the Oven to Table chapter (pages 21–45) you can simply throw things in a pan, stick it in the oven and more or less walk away. If you're still getting the hang of cooking, ignore most of the 'extra' advice. Faster than Delivery (pages 46–83) is also a good place to begin, as you'll become more familiar with using the condiments and ingredients listed to maximise taste with minimal time and effort. Plus, these recipes are so easy that you'll surprise yourself and any guests, with what you've pulled together. I always tend to feel quite pleased with myself after creating a beautiful 20-minute meal. Once you've mastered the main

recipes, you can start reading the side notes and swap-outs to get an idea of how the recipe can be adjusted. But only go there once you feel ready, so you don't become overwhelmed. Whatever your level, read the below information before you start.

Swapping proteins
In the Salad for Dinner chapter (pages 119–141), most of the recipes have instructions on how to cook basic proteins such as scallops, steak, prawns (shrimp) and chicken. The idea is that you can also use these proteins for the other dishes, for instance, subbing in chicken for prawns, if you just had prawns the other night or aren't in the mood. The recipes are fluid, so don't feel constricted by what you see written on the page.

Quality matters
As every chef I've ever interviewed has hammered into my head, the end result will only be as good as the ingredients that you start with. This means not only using high-quality oils, fats and salts, but also using ingredients that are in season and fresh because they taste better. You're fighting an uphill battle if you start with lifeless, sad-looking vegetables – yes, I'm talking about that limp, squishy squash you found in the back of your fridge. I don't like wasting food either, but that's a no-go.

Stick to the seasons

In this day and age, it's easy to get raspberries and strawberries year-round, but they also don't taste nearly as good as they do in the height of the summer season where you feel like they are infused with the flavours of the sun, sweet and sticky juices dripping down your hands as you eat them. For this reason, when applicable, the recipes have seasonal swap outs.

Most importantly...

Have fun. My friend Jon makes endless fun of me because I use this word a lot. For example, 'Want to take a fun walk?' or 'Should we get a fun drink?' As if it wouldn't be fun, if I didn't say the word. I hope that you do what makes you feel good while making these recipes, whether it's lighting candles, putting on music, dancing around while you wait for something to roast or simply sitting on the couch with a glass of wine until your timer goes off (on that note, timers are very helpful, especially if there are other people around to distract you). I have a hula hoop in the kitchen that I often use while I'm waiting for something to finish cooking. Nothing is right and nothing is wrong – just go with what makes you happy.

Serving sizes and sharing

Most of the recipes in this book have been created for 2 people to have a full dinner, plus seconds and/or leftovers. But as, I'm big on casual entertaining, it can be fun to make a few dishes and graze with family and friends. In that case, the dishes should serve 4, with an added salad or side dish.

RECIPE ICONS

Efficiency moves
This icon is meant to help you tackle the recipe at hand. It tells you where to start and what to do to maximise your time. They're by no means something you need to follow if they stress you out. Remember that this is meant to be fun.

Recipe notes
This icon will give you added information that is helpful for completing the recipe, make sure to pay attention to these!

Ingredient swaps and variations
Sometimes a recipe will be just as delicious with another ingredient swapped in, or by making a small tweak in a preparation to make things a bit different.

Leftover notes
Look to these notes for innovative ways to make the most of leftovers or the best way to reheat them.

I once published an interview series with chefs about what was in their fridge. From then on, I've daydreamed that one day someone would ask me, 'Yasmin, what ingredients are always in your fridge?' I'd be ready with: 'Parmesan, Bulgarian feta, tons of Asian condiments and eggs. Outside of the fridge, I always have garlic, lemons and onions.' (No one has asked.)

In addition to the ones above, having the below items stocked in your pantry will come in handy when cooking from this book so that you can whip up any of the dishes quickly and efficiently:

Chillies
It's typically the seeds and membrane inside chillies that carry the majority of the heat, which won't dissipate with cooking. So, if you're sensitive to heat, then always remove those parts for the recipes, as some include them whole without seeding them.

Coconut milk
Delicious and essential for a successful curry, I tend to opt for the lighter version, which still provides a creamy richness to dishes without the extra fat and calories.

Curry powder
Perfect for our purposes, curry powder is a blend of up to 20 different spices. The hotter kind is called Madras, and the less hot is usually just 'curry powder'.

Dijon mustard
I once went to a restaurant in Hong Kong that served steak with a sampling of mustards; it was incredible. While mustard comes in many fabulous varieties, to keep things simple, have Dijon mustard in the fridge as it can be used in a range of recipes from simple pan sauces to dressings.

Fish sauce
A popular condiment in South East Asian cuisine, it has a strong taste and pungent smell as it's typically made from fermented fish. Because of this, it's an easy way to add a bit of umami (savouriness), which is why it's found in a few of the recipes in this book.

Ground cumin
Earthy and aromatic, cumin is used a lot in Middle Eastern and Mediterranean cooking. This is one of my favourites as you'll see, and I fly through a supply of it.

Harissa
A Tunisian sauce that's typically made from hot chillies, garlic, olive oil, plus cumin and other spices. It's usually served with couscous, but, as you'll see in the following recipes, it can be used in sauces, soups and as a marinade.

Parmesan rind
You know after you've used a wedge of Parmesan and you've whittled it down to the rind, or you were really bad at wrapping it so it's a bit dried out? Well, in either of those cases, don't throw it out. Save the rinds for whenever you make your next sauce, soup or pasta. Add one as the last ingredient before simmering and take out before you serve.

Passata

Passata (strained tomatoes) are crushed and strained tomatoes usually without any seasoning. It provides a smooth texture and intense tomato taste. The sizes of these bottles vary, which is why I call for a specific measurement rather than listed by tin or jar.

Pasta and noodles

Stock your shelves with dried spaghetti and penne (usually one long one and one tubular one works) and soba, ramen and/or rice noodles for quick, impromptu meals. They require minimal cooking and are easy ways to make a meal more substantial in a pinch.

Saffron

This expensive spice adds a beautiful golden-sunset hue to dishes and an intoxicating aroma – because it is so pricey, the best way to use it is to create a saffron water by grinding a tiny bit of the threads, into a powder and mixing with hot water. This way, one purchase will last a long time.

Sambal

This is a hot chilli sauce that's typically found in Indonesian cuisine. It's great way to add heat to soups, noodle dishes and marinades but is also good to serve as a condiment.

Soy sauce

I call for the low-salt version in these recipes.

Storing dried spices and herbs

Dried spices and herbs should be kept in a cool, dark place (read: not above the stove) and will lose their potency in about six months. I know, you all probably have spices that have been in your cupboard for two years or more. You can revive them a bit by toasting them in a dry frying pan, but, if you're wondering why dishes don't have as much flavour or taste as you'd like, then this might be one reason why.

Tahini

This is a thick paste made from ground sesame seeds – you've more than likely eaten it in hummus – and I use it a lot in dressings.

Thai curry pastes

A blend of spices and chillies, they are typically found in green or red (usually a little hotter than green) varieties.

Wakame/nori

Wakame is the silky seaweed that you find in miso soup. It comes dehydrated and cooks quickly in stocks, so you don't need to rehydrate it before cooking, even if it says it on the instructions. You can throw wakame into quick noodle or soup dishes for a little more substance and a heartier meal. Toasted nori (another type of dried seaweed) is good as a topping for adding crunch and salty bites of flavour, too.

White miso

Used a lot in Japanese cuisine, miso is a fermented bean paste that comes in different varieties. Lighter coloured ones, like white miso, are used in more delicate dishes and can be used in all of the recipes in this book. Low-salt options are available, if you're sensitive to it. It's great in salad dressings, marinades and soups.

GOOD TO KNOW WORDS AND PHRASES

The below words and phrases took me a long time to fully understand; maybe this is a shortcoming on my part, as some of you might find these cues quite obvious. If anyone else shares my former confusion about them, then I sincerely hope this saves you some time and head-scratching. Plus, you'll be seeing them over and over again in these recipes, so you can always refer back here for a little extra guidance. This is what I mean when I say...

Until shimmering

When adding oil to a pan, wait until you see glimmering ripples on the surface of the oil and that it looks like the ocean glistening under the sunlight. That's when you add in your first ingredient(s).

Until lightly smoking

This is when there is a little genie-like waft of smoke coming from the pan. Cast iron pans emit this whiteish dancing vision without the addition of oil.

Until fragrant

As in, 'add the garlic and spices, cook until fragrant, about 30 seconds'. For years I would write that cue and not really know what it meant, other than that one of my editors had added it into my recipe. That was until I put a ton of whole spices into hot ghee while making kitchari and the fragrance hit me – there was no way not to understand that cue when warming, rich aromas were wafting through the air. Maybe I was using old spices or maybe not enough spice to really smell it, but, ideally, you should be able to smell the spices infusing into whatever fat you're using, whether it's oil, butter or ghee. If not, stick to the 30-second rule until you have the epiphany that I did.

Until soft

As in, 'add the shallot, salt and cook until soft'. Shallots, onions and others in that family will release liquid when salt has been added, so this refers to that process. And it also means that it will feel physically soft as you stir with a wooden spoon.

Stirring frequently

You're standing over the pot, wooden spoon or other utensil in hand, perhaps a drink in the other, keeping an eye on the pot/pan, stirring every 30 seconds or so.

Stirring occasionally

Same as above, but you can turn your back to get another ingredient or quickly check your phone/ upload a photo. Stir every minute or two.

Gentle simmer

Little bubbles are breaking on the surface in an easy-going, not rapid-fire way. There should just be a few bubbles in the middle of the liquid's surface.

Active simmer

Little bubbles are breaking in rapid-fire across the surface of the liquid (not just in the middle), but they should be on the smaller side – the heat level will be lower than an active boil. You want to cook rice and tomato sauce at an active simmer.

Active boil

Kind of like when you're taking a bath and the water hits the bubble bath liquid and the bubbles go a bit crazy. Same but a little different – the surface should be covered in bubbles that keep forming. Most of the time you'll bring the liquid to an active boil and then reduce to an active simmer.

Vigorous boil

These are the massive, rolling bubbles across the surface that seem a little scary, almost like they are going to explode or erupt, so you'll need to watch over this. This is mostly for cooking pasta.

Until al dente

This means 'firm to the bite' in Italian. You should be able to take a bite through and see only a tiny amount of starchy white parts, and there should be a little give against your teeth. If it's soft, then you've let the pasta cook a touch too long. Unless you like it that way. Sometimes, I'll say, 'just before al dente', which means that it should feel a little too tough to bite through and not tasty. This way, when you finish cooking the pasta in the sauce, it will be al dente when done.

Reduce

This refers to when you add liquid to a pan, usually to deglaze, which is a term that describes scraping up the caramelised brown bits on the bottom of the pan with a wooden spoon. Typically, you want the liquid to cook down and reduce in volume. You should be able to see the other ingredients in the bottom of the pan with just a little liquid left, unless specified otherwise.

Roughly torn

This usually refers to herbs or leafy greens. Instead of chopping, take the washed herbs in your hand and tear them directly over the plate, pan or whatever you're putting them on or into.

Garlic cloves and onions

Garlic cloves can vary in size drastically. We are only calling for small cloves in this book. Sub one large clove for two small ones. Same goes for onions – I'll call for either small or medium-sized ones in these recipes. A small onion is roughly 150 g (5 oz), so half of a sliced one will equal to about 75 g (2.5 oz/½ cup). A large one is roughly 225 g (8 oz), and half of one is 85 g (3 oz/¾ cup) sliced.

Juice of lemon or lime

Once, when making margaritas for a friend's family, their father said, 'I have never seen someone get so much juice out a lime'. This is because of a trick my parents taught me. You take a fork, stick the tines in a halved lemon or lime, and then use a lever motion to move the fork back and inside the citrus half, while squeezing it onto the fork – this really gets every last drop out. Plus, I find it a lot easier than using a citrus juicer (less clean up), and it's kind of fun. So when recipes call for the juice of lemon or lime, that's the level of juice that's expected. But, as always, add to taste. It should roughly equate to 2 tablespoons of juice from 1 lemon and 1 tablespoon of juice from 1 lime, if you need a visual indication.

Adjust seasoning

Regularly taste your dish while it's cooking and ask yourself if the seasoning needs to be adjusted. Do it with purpose and intention rather then as a habit.

HELPFUL THINGS TO KNOW IN THE KITCHEN

The benefits of citrus

One of the more valuable things that Kenji López-Alt, my editor at Serious Eats, told me as both a recipe developer and professional eater, was that many dishes taste unbalanced because they are lacking in acid. Always make sure to add a little acid to a dish (with the exception of tomato-based ones as tomatoes are already acidic) before adding more salt or other seasonings. And, if you happen to oversalt something, acid is a quick way to cover it.

To crush nuts or peppercorns

Place them in a clean tea towel and fold over all sides so that they can't escape. Then, on a durable surface, use the back of a frying pan (skillet) to gently smash them.

To toast seeds or nuts

Heat the seeds in a dry frying pan over a medium heat, shaking the pan every 30 seconds or so, until you hear the seeds start to crackle and pop or they have darkened in colour. Remove from heat and let cool.

Cutting spring onions (scallions) on a bias

This makes the meal look a lot prettier and all you have to do is hold the spring onion at an angle when you cut it so that the cut pieces also look angled. You're welcome.

How to prep lemongrass

Trim the ends, peel off the outer layers with your fingers – they wrap around and are easy to peel, promise, just keep going until you reach a softer, paler inside – that's the part we want to chop, grate or mince.

How to crumble feta

You'll need this tip for a lot of recipes in this book (see I Have a Thing for Feta, page 106). Place the feta on a cutting board and use the back of a fork to press down on it, moving along the block pieces as if you were knocking down a building.

Cutting butternut squash

Butternut can be a pain to cut (I always feel like I'm going to lose a finger doing it), so if buying pre-cut squash makes your life easier, then by all means, do it. Otherwise, here are some tips for you.

1. Cut off the top and bottom.

2. Peel the outside.

3. Cut in half lengthwise and scoop out the seeds.

4. Cut the base and top in half.

5. Chop into cubes.

Greens for swapping

Kale/mustard greens/beetroot (beet) greens/chard/ spring (collard) greens/cime di rapa (broccoli rabe)/ spinach/turnip greens – add these early in the cooking process as they take a little longer to wilt and cook. With the exception of spinach, most of these greens run on the bitter side, which means they need a little extra attention. While you could blanch them, that just feels like a giant pain in the arse. My go-to moves for cooking these greens are using strong spices or ingredients such as cumin, chilli flakes or sausage and then making sure there is acid to finish off the dish (such as lemon, lime or a vinegar) and salt. A fat, such as cheese, also never hurts (see Garlicky charred greens with wholewheat penne, page 92).

Baby rocket (arugula)/baby spinach – these greens can be stirred in during the last 2 minutes of cooking or even off heat as they wilt quickly. You'll notice spinach significantly wilts down, and almost disappears after a few minutes, so don't feel overwhelmed when you're first adding it in. I promise it will work out.

Roasting vegetables

Vegetables are typically done when you can pierce the thickest part easily with a fork, and they have a nice brown char on them; this is the flavour-maker, so don't skimp on this part by taking them out too early. With that said, the jump from nicely charred to blackened and inedible is pretty quick, so once you see that browning start, stay close and keep an eye on it.

TOOLS

There's not a lot you actually need to make these recipes, as I'm a minimalist in the kitchen, even though I have a lot of fancy equipment (including a Vitamix that I bought on a whim with credit card points). I rarely use it, mostly because I stopped making almond milk once I moved out of Los Angeles, and I'm too lazy to clean it. Below, though, are a few tips on the equipment you'll be using in this book.

Baking tray (sheet pan)
Purchasing a durable and heavy one so that it stays flat and even is key. The size is essential (23 x 33 cm/ 9 x 13 in) so that the foods can spread out evenly without overcrowding and will brown rather than steam. Opt for one with a small rim so that any juices that are released stay on the baking tray. A lot of ovens are not evenly heated, and this means that one or more parts of the baking tray will be cooked more than others. For this reason, it's important to rotate halfway through so items cook evenly.

Fan (convection) ovens
If you have one of these, then your cooking times might be slightly reduced (by about 10°C/50°F) for many of these recipes, as these are intended and tested for home ovens without fan assistance. Make sure to take that into account – on a positive note, it's a good test for you to learn when food is done by look, feel and taste rather than time alone.

Know your grill (broiler)
Like ovens, the grills that live inside are not made the same. One would think that timing instructions for a grill would be ubiquitous, but they are not. The older oven in my apartment has a slower, less forceful grill. Expensive and modern ovens will have grills that are akin to salamanders in restaurants and will burn food to ashes in the same time it takes my oven to get it lightly charred. This is not meant to scare you, but rather to encourage you to get to know your grill. It's good to keep an eye on it regardless. If you have one of the slower variety, then the timings in this book will work well. If you are lucky enough to have a fab oven, then keep a watchful eye on the food to avoid burning, and keep pulling out the rack to check every 30 seconds.

Microplane grater
This is the best thing for grating garlic, ginger, cheese and citrus zest. It's an incredible multi-functional tool that is used for most of the recipes in this book. Opt for the coarse grater as you can use it for the most things.

Cast iron pan
You'll want something that can be used on the hob (stovetop) and then transferred to the oven. A 30 cm (12 in) cast iron pan is perfect for this and not very expensive; plus, if well taken care of, it can last a lifetime or more.

Digital thermometer
This probably seems really gadgety, and I felt the same way, until I was given one to test out when I was an editor, and, I must say, I fell in love with it. I used to always be so fearful about undercooking chicken or overcooking meat, especially when guests were over, and this took all that worry out if it. With that said, all of the meat recipes have been timed and prepared in ways that are foolproof and easy, so you will still be fine if you don't want to buy one.

Flameproof casserole dish (Dutch oven)
Ask for one for a holiday or birthday present because they can be used for braises, soups, pastas and anything that needs to be transferred to the oven. Plus, they're beautiful to serve in and make for one less dish to wash.

OVEN
TO
TABLE

Go-to weeknight pizza (page 24)

SET IT AND
FORGET IT

(KIND OF)

I once went to this fabulous pizza cooking class in New York to write an article with pizza-making tips and ended up having a great time. The teacher was so lively and fun, with an infectious passion for making pizza – the kind of person that makes you excited to do whatever they are doing because of the enthusiasm they exude. We made our own pizza dough from scratch, learned how to roll it out on our knuckles so that gravity would help us stretch it, and then got to eat a lot of pizza while drinking red wine, aka my ideal night. I left giddy, happy and both emboldened and empowered: I remember thinking on the way home, I'm always going to make my own pizzas from now on; this is so easy and fabulous!

I did not do that, in fact. Not once.

So, when it came to making the pizzas in this section, I decided to forgo all of the worry about making dough, using a pizza stone, pizza peel, flour, etc., that stopped me from repeating that lovely experience at home and make it simple and quick so you can still experience the joy of having a pizza party without the stress and mess. This approach extends to the entire chapter – not just the Go-to weeknight pizza (page 24) – in which you essentially put a few things on a baking tray (sheet pan), slide it into the oven and walk away until it's done. Some dishes, like the Mozzarella-topped chicken cutlets (page 38), are done in 20 minutes and look and taste like something that should take way longer.

I like cooking directly on the tray and don't love using kitchen foil, but you can use that or baking parchment (not wax paper, which will burn) for most of the recipes if you want an even easier clean up.

You'll have a decent amount of downtime, so don't forget to put on some good music, enjoy some wine and surround yourself with fun people you love – that usually makes most things better.

GO-TO WEEKNIGHT PIZZA

Serves 2, 4 for sharing
Prep 10 minutes
Total 35 minutes

2 tablespoons olive oil

450 g (1 lb) shop-bought fresh or frozen pizza dough, at room temperature

250 g (9 oz/1 cup) passata (strained tomatoes)

1 garlic clove, grated or minced

1 teaspoon dried oregano

½ teaspoon dried red chilli flakes, plus more for sprinkling

salt and freshly ground black pepper

225 g (8 oz) mozzarella, torn into small, bite-sized chunks

75 g (2½ oz/½ cup) grated Parmesan

15 g (½ oz/½ cup) basil leaves and fine stems, sliced or roughly torn

extra-virgin olive oil, for drizzling

✎ Most pizza recipes ask you to make a sauce separately, which we are skipping to save time by using passata (strained tomatoes) (page 11).

If you're lucky enough to live in a city with great pizza shops, then ask if you can buy their dough. Alternatively, buy frozen dough from your supermarket and make sure to take it out the morning you want to make your pizza.

This is a great weeknight meal for the winter when it's enjoyable to get your kitchen steamy, and on the weekend when you're having a lazy one and just want to watch movies, eat food and drink wine all day. It's fun to do with friends: double the recipe for two pizzas, put on the sauce, then each person gets a half to do as they will. Eat the first while the second one cooks. Share and compare thoughts on each other's choices (obviously in a loving and constructive fashion). Repeat as needed for more friends.

⏱ Take the pizza dough out of the fridge (hopefully you removed the frozen pizza dough that morning or night before) when you first get home or up to an hour before you want to cook it. Use this time to do chores, or whatever else you feel like. Then get the ingredients together. Clean up and set the table while the pizza cooks.

Method

1. Preheat the oven to 230°C (450°F/Gas 8).

2. Grease the baking tray (sheet pan) with olive oil to prevent the pizza from sticking, using your hands to thoroughly coat the surface until they can glide easily across it.

3. Gently press the dough out with the pads of your fingertips, stretching it out to the edges of each tray or as close as you can get (don't stress about this too much). Make sure to patch any holes by folding the dough on itself – also not the end of the world if it's not perfect. If the dough feels very springy and won't stretch, then cover it with cling film (plastic wrap) for 10–30 minutes, at room temperature – this allows the gluten to relax so you can stretch it more easily. It's almost magical how different the dough feels when you do this.

4. Measure the passata in a measuring cup, then stir in the garlic, oregano, chilli flakes, mixing with a spoon and seasoning to taste with salt and pepper. Then spread the tomato mixture on the dough, leaving a little space at the edges.

Optional Toppings

→ *For mushroom and jalapeño pizza:* top the sauced pizza before it goes into the oven with 75 g (2½ oz/1 cup) sliced chestnut (cremini) or button mushrooms and 1 thinly sliced chilli, then continue as per the recipe.

For Italian sausage with ricotta pizza: top the sauced pizza before it goes in the oven with 1–2 uncooked sausages, removed from their casing and pulled into small bit-sized pieces and 250 g (9 oz/1 cup) ricotta, drained and lightly salted (use instead of mozzarella), finish with the Parmesan, then continue as per the recipe.

For salad pizza: make the pizza, then, when it comes out of the oven, lightly dress 2 cups of baby rocket (arugula) with ½ tablespoon extra-virgin olive oil, salt and pepper (you can shave some extra Parmesan on there as well). Top on the pizza and serve with a fork and knife (or not).

5. Spread the chunks of mozzarella evenly around, leaving some space between them as they will melt and spread out. Top with Parmesan.

6. Bake in the oven until the cheese has melted and the crusts are golden brown, about 15–20 minutes. If your oven is uneven or you're unsure, then turn the tray halfway through cooking. Remove and let cool for 5 minutes. Prep the basil and any other toppings, then finish with basil, chilli flakes and a drizzle of olive oil, if desired, and cut with a chef's knife or pizza wheel and serve.

See photo on pages 20–21

WAKEY, WAKEY, CHEESY EGGS AND BAKEY

Serves 4 for dinner
Prep 10 minutes
Total 30 minutes

---

225 g (8 oz/8 slices) bacon

150 g (5 oz/1 cup) baby plum (grape) tomatoes, halved

salt and freshly ground black pepper

olive oil, for greasing

8 eggs

½ teaspoon dried red chilli flakes, or more as desired

75 g (2½ oz/½ cup) drained and lightly salted ricotta, crumbled feta or grated Parmesan

toast, for serving

1 ripe Hass avocado, halved, destoned, peeled and sliced, for serving

juice of 1 lime

rocket (arugula), for serving (optional)

hot sauce, for serving

/ To check if the eggs are done, gently jiggle the ramekin: the yolks should move a little and bounce back, while the whites will be steady. The sides of the eggs will be bubbling and firm (they cook the quickest) and will start to brown when it's close to time. If they are still super jiggly, then give it another 30 seconds and check again.

➡ Add chopped spinach, mushrooms or other veg to the bottom of the ramekin (no more than 4 tablespoons) and layer the eggs on top.

Since I was four, my family has been going to the same place in Maine, USA, every summer. It's a time to unwind, be in nature and go off the grid. My dad orders the same breakfast every day of the trip, and, inevitably, mid-way through the week, the server says, 'The usual for you?' He orders two eggs 'over easy', bacon and a side of pancakes. No toast.

This recipe is inspired by that meal, but with my own twist. It's an easy one for when you can't be bothered to think too much – and a way to cook bacon evenly without any mess. The tomatoes cook in the rendered bacon fat, infusing them with a delicious salty flavour. Scoop them up with toast or place on the eggs.

Method

1. Preheat the oven to 190°C (375°F/Gas 5).

2. Place the bacon in the middle of a baking tray (sheet pan), spread the tomatoes around, topping them with a pinch of salt and pepper, then place 4 lightly oiled ramekins on the outer edges of the baking tray. The tomatoes will cook in the rendered bacon fat, so no need for oil.

3. Crack 2 eggs inside each ramekin and season with salt, pepper, chilli flakes, if desired, and top with your choice of cheese.

4. Carefully place in the oven (the ramekins might try and slide around), and cook until the bacon is crispy and the egg whites are set and yolks are runny, about 18–20 minutes, turning the tray around in the oven halfway through to ensure even cooking. If the bacon is cooked before the eggs, then remove and drain on a paper towel-lined plate.

5. Meanwhile, set the table, climb into comfy clothes and make some toast, if you want to dip it into the eggs (you should). Near the finish time, slice the avocado, top it with salt and a squeeze of lime juice and divide it between the plates with the rocket and toast.

6. Carefully remove the baking tray from the oven, place the ramekins on plates (they are hot, so watch out) and divvy up the bacon and tomatoes, garnishing the eggs with rocket, if desired, and serving with avocado, hot sauce and toast.

OVEN TO TABLE

MISO-GHEE CHICKEN

WITH ROASTED RADISHES

Serves 2, 4 for sharing
Prep 5 minutes
Total 35 minutes

---

4 skin-on, bone-in chicken thighs (about 657 g/1 lb 8 oz)

salt and freshly ground black pepper

2 teaspoons olive oil, divided

1½ teaspoons miso paste

1 tablespoon ghee, at room temperature

450 g (1 lb) radishes, ends trimmed and halved, smaller ones kept whole

juice of 1 lime

2 spring onions (scallions), light green and white parts only, sliced

black or white sesame seeds, for sprinkling (optional)

Radishes, available year round, end up tasting more like potatoes when roasted and lose their spiciness, which makes this a light weeknight meal that still leaves you satisfied.

Ghee is butter that's been clarified and then cooked again to caramelise it, which results in an intoxicating nutty aroma when heated (just wait for it). For these reasons, it works well with high-heat cooking, such as roasting and frying.

I love tossing this miso ghee over soba noodles with spring onions (scallions), herbs and stir-fried greens for a quick dinner.

My life significantly changed after I began seeing a holistic facialist. She was able to look at my skin and could immediately tell what I had and hadn't been eating, and what was going on in my emotional life. I would be more than happy to go on about everything I've learned from her over the years, but I suppose the relevant one here is cooking with ghee. This miso ghee is a lactose-free compound butter that infuses the chicken as it cooks, keeping it moist and tender – I use a similar trick to keep roast turkey breast moist.

Make the miso-ghee mixture and prep the chicken. You can do this up to an hour ahead, if you have the time. Cut the radishes while the chicken is in the oven. You'll have some downtime to clean up.

Method

1. Preheat the oven to 230°C (450°F/Gas 8) with one rack in the middle of the oven, and one 15 cm (6 in) from the heat source (if your grill (broiler) is inside of your oven).

2. Season the chicken all over with salt, pepper and half of the oil. In a mixing bowl, mash together the miso paste and ghee until combined. Lift up the skin on the chicken thigh, carefully creating a space between the skin and meat and place a little mound of miso-ghee inside. Close the pocket, and lightly press on top of the skin to spread it around. Repeat for the other pieces. Massage any remaining miso-ghee mixture all over the chicken, leaving behind 1 teaspoon in the bowl. Place the chicken skin-side up on a baking tray (sheet pan) and place in the oven. Set a timer for 15 minutes.

3. In the same mixing bowl, toss the radishes with the remaining miso-ghee mixture, 1 teaspoon of the oil, salt and pepper. Remove the tray when the timer goes off and scatter the radishes around the chicken, cooking until they are tender and lightly browned, and chicken is cooked through, or until the temperature in the thickest part of the thigh reaches 75°C (165°F), about 10–15 minutes more. If the chicken skin is not as browned as you'd like, then grill until the skin is crispy and golden, about 1–2 minutes. Squeeze the lime juice over chicken and radishes, then garnish with the spring onions and sesame seeds, if using. Divide between plates and serve.

See photo overleaf

OVEN TO TABLE

LEMON-SAFFRON CHICKEN KEBABS

Serves 2, 4 for sharing
Prep 10 minutes
Total 25 minutes

½ teaspoon saffron threads

1 tablespoon warm water

2 tablespoons low-fat Greek yoghurt
  or skyr

juice of 2 lemons

salt and freshly ground black pepper

675 g (1 lb 8 oz) skinless boneless
  chicken thighs, cut into 5 cm
  (2 in) chunks

2 medium-sized tomatoes, left whole
  or quartered

1 small red onion, halved and cut into
  2.5 cm (1 in) slices

1 tablespoon olive oil

1–2 large pieces lavash or pitta bread,
  lightly toasted, for serving

fresh herbs such as mint, basil and
  parsley, for serving

75 g (2½ oz/½ cup) feta (preferably
  Bulgarian), crumbled, for serving

🖊 You can skewer the chicken
and vegetables for a more visually
appealing presentation. Make sure to
soak wooden or bamboo skewers in
warm water for 10–30 minutes before
cooking so that they don't burn.

➦ Substitute the saffron threads
for 1 tablespoon ground turmeric.
No water needed.

This is a variation of a traditional Persian chicken kebab that uses yoghurt to help tenderise the chicken, which is great for getting dinner on the table quickly. You can marinate the chicken the night before, then pop it in the oven when you get home, if you like. I also tested it with just 15 minutes in the marinade, and it was delicious, so don't stress if you can't do it ahead of time – it'll be good either way.

⏱ If you can, immediately marinate the chicken when you get home, change, tidy up, watch a TV show and try to give it as much time as possible, as the flavour gets better the longer it sits in the marinade. Otherwise make the marinade, then prep the vegetables so it has a little time. Toast the bread while the chicken is cooking or place on another baking tray (sheet pan) in the oven to heat up.

Method

1. In a shallow bowl, add the saffron threads and crush them into a powder using the back or bottom of a wooden spoon. Mix with the water, stirring until mostly dissolved. Mix in the yoghurt and lemon juice and season with salt and pepper. Add the chicken and coat well with the marinade. Let sit in the fridge for up to 24 hours or a minimum of 15 minutes.

2. Preheat the grill (broiler) with the rack 15 cm (6 in) from the heat source (if it's located inside of your oven). Place the tomatoes and onion on one side of a baking tray (sheet pan) and toss with the olive oil, salt and pepper. Set the chicken pieces on the other side and put under the grill. Cook until the top of the chicken starts to look slightly charred, about 6–7 minutes, depending on the strength of your grill. Remove the baking tray and turn over the chicken pieces, tomatoes and onion, then return to the grill until the chicken is cooked through and reaches 75°C (165°F) in the thickest part of the meat, about 6–7 minutes more. (There should be no pink visible or squishy, glassy-looking part in the middle of the chicken.) The tomato skins should be blistered and charred in spots and the onions will be a deeper purple hue and silky in texture.

3. Remove and serve with the tomatoes and onions, toasted lavash, fresh herbs and some feta to make little sandwiches.

See photo overleaf

ROASTED HALIBUT
WITH LEMON, TOMATOES AND HERBS

Serves 4
Prep 10 minutes
Total 25 minutes

4 x 170 g (6 oz) skinless halibut or
  other white fish fillets (about 4 cm/
  1½ in thick)

600 g (1 lb 5 oz/4 cups) baby plum
  (grape) tomatoes, halved

2 organic lemons, 1 with ends trimmed
  and sliced into rounds, 1 zested

2 garlic cloves, grated or minced

salt and freshly ground black pepper

½ teaspoon of dried red chilli flakes

3 tablespoons olive oil

4–6 rosemary or thyme sprigs

2 tablespoons extra-virgin olive oil

1 teaspoon capers, drained and
  chopped

15 g (½ oz/½ cup) fresh parsley leaves
  and fine stems, roughly chopped

crusty bread, for serving

Now, I know some of you might think, oh this roasted lemon looks pretty, but you're going to push it to the side of your plate and not eat it. Understandable, because eating lemon rinds isn't a common thing. However, let me just say that you will be pleasantly surprised by the soft, flavourful rind – plus, it's part of what makes this dish so great. I note buying organic because of this eating intention. If you are as stubborn as I can be sometimes and refuse to listen despite perhaps knowing deep down that I might be right, then you can squeeze a bit of lemon juice on the fish when it comes out of the oven to balance it out (use the roasted lemons to do this).

⏱ Preheat the oven, pat dry the fish, cut the tomatoes and prep the garlic, then mix everything together on the roasting tin. You'll most likely be done as the oven comes to temperature or shortly after. Make the parsley topping while the fish cooks and also use that time to set the table, pour the wine and cut up the bread.

Method

1. Preheat the oven to 200°C (400°F/Gas 6) with the rack in the middle of the oven.

2. Place the fish in a roasting tin with the tomatoes, sliced lemon and garlic then season with salt, pepper and chilli flakes. Coat the ingredients with the oil so they have a light sheen to them. Place the fillets in the middle, skinned-side down. Place a sprig of rosemary or thyme on top of each fillet. Sprinkle any loose rosemary or other sprigs on the other ingredients.

3. Place in the oven and cook until the fish is opaque and flakes easily when touched, about 15 minutes.

4. Meanwhile, in a small mixing bowl, combine the extra-virgin olive oil, capers, parsley and lemon zest and season to taste with salt and pepper.

5. When the fish is cooked, remove from the oven and divide between plates along with the tomatoes and lemon rounds. Finish each fish with the parsley mixture and pepper. Serve with crusty bread.

SAMBAL-ROASTED CHICKEN THIGHS

Serves 2, 4 for sharing
Prep 5 minutes
Total 45 minutes

---

4 skin-on, bone-in chicken thighs (about 675 g/1 lb 8 oz)

salt and freshly ground black pepper

1 teaspoon fresh ginger, grated or minced, from a 5 cm (2 in) piece

2 garlic cloves, grated or minced

2 tablespoons sambal oelek

2 tablespoons low-salt soy sauce

1 teaspoon brown sugar

1 tablespoon sesame oil

1 teaspoon fish sauce

4 spring onions (scallions), tops and ends trimmed

600 g (1 lb 5 oz/4 cups) green beans, ends trimmed

150 g (5 oz/2 cups) chestnut (cremini) or button mushrooms, trimmed and quartered

1 tablespoon olive oil

---

*You can make the marinade the night before and leave the chicken in a sealed bag or covered bowl for up to 24 hours.

Fresh, unpeeled ginger can be frozen for up to six weeks in the freezer. Wrap it tightly, cut off the amount you want to use, then return the rest.

One summer weekend at my family home we had leftover steamed lobsters from dinner the night before, so I figured I would make a lobster *all'arrabbiata* of sorts. My dad picked a red chilli from his plant and said, 'watch out, this one might be hot'. I cut off the tip and carefully took a bite. Pshh, it was fine. I seeded it, sliced it in half and cooked it along with the sauce in case it was secretly spicy. Well, the pasta came out fantastically. My dad fished out the pepper to toss away, but I boldly proclaimed, 'it's not that hot', and proceeded to cut off a huge piece to eat. I was wrong. Very, very wrong. In fact, I was unable to eat the rest of the pasta. This dish is not *that* hot, but if it were being discussed via text message, I'd be sending you three fire emojis right now.

Method

1. Preheat the oven to 230°C (450°F/Gas 8) with one rack in the middle of the oven and one 15 cm (6 in) from the heat source (if your grill (broiler) is inside your oven).

2. Season the chicken generously with salt and pepper. In a shallow mixing bowl, combine the ginger, garlic, sambal, soy sauce, sugar, sesame oil and fish sauce until the sugar is mostly dissolved. Add the chicken and coat well with sauce.

3. Place the chicken skin-side up on a baking tray (sheet pan) and slide onto the middle rack. Set a timer for 10 minutes. Meanwhile, place the vegetables in the same bowl without wiping it out, and toss with the olive oil, salt, pepper and remaining marinade.

4. After 10 minutes remove the chicken from the oven, and spread the vegetables between the chicken pieces. Turn the tray, return to oven and cook until the green beans are blistered, the mushrooms are browned and the chicken skin is a golden brown and reaches 75°C (165°F) in the thickest part of the meat, about 20–25 minutes more. About halfway, vigorously shake the tray a little so that the green beans move around.

5. If the chicken skin is not quite as golden as you'd like, then turn on the grill and grill until the skin is crispy and browned, about 1–3 minutes, depending on the strength of your broiler (keep an eye on it so it doesn't burn). The green beans will also get a little more blistered, so remove if already done to your preference (taste and see). Remove from the heat and serve.

BAKED FETA
WITH GREENS AND LEMON-TAHINI DRESSING

Serves 2, 4 for sharing
Prep 5 minutes
Total 25 minutes

---

400 g (15 oz) tin chickpeas (garbanzo beans), drained and rinsed

300 g (10½ oz) red or curly kale, or cavolo nero (lacinato kale), leaves removed from stems, cut or hand torn into 5 cm (2 in) pieces (about 3 packed cups)

3 tablespoons olive oil, plus more for drizzling

salt and freshly ground black pepper

1 teaspoon smoked paprika

¼ teaspoon cayenne pepper

2 x 200 g (8 oz) blocks feta, preferably Bulgarian, halved horizontally to make 3 cm (1 in) thick pieces

30 g (1 oz/¼ cup) pumpkin seeds

1 tablespoon tahini

3 tablespoons extra-virgin olive oil

juice of 3 lemons

✏ If you are not into feta (we can talk about this later), try halloumi and cut it into small cubes. Halloumi is a brined cheese with a high melting point, which makes it easy to grill, fry or bake without it falling apart. The only downside is that if you let it cool too long, it gets rubbery in texture.

🧊 The next day, mix leftovers with scrambled eggs or use on top of cooked grains with the dressing.

There aren't many times when I think that feta can get better than it is in its natural state (page 106). It already adds a tangy creaminess to dishes, so it almost feels selfish to ask more of it. And yet, when you bake it, it transforms into something different – not better but, just as good. It becomes softer, both in texture and taste, and feels like a more gentle way to eat feta, if that makes sense. Plus, the leftovers are solid.

⏱ Preheat the oven while you prep the chickpeas (garbanzo beans) and kale. Make the dressing while the food is in the oven.

Method

1. Preheat the oven to 200°C (400°F/Gas 6) with a baking tray (sheet pan) inside.

2. When the oven is ready, remove the baking tray and carefully add the chickpeas and kale, then toss with the oil, salt, pepper and spices, using a wooden spoon or your hands, making sure not to burn yourself. Spread the ingredients evenly, then create little pockets to nestle the feta into, making sure they have direct contact with the baking tray. Drizzle the feta with olive oil and pepper.

3. Return to the oven and bake until feta has softened, the kale has browned in spots and the chickpeas become crisp with a darker brown hue – around 15–20 minutes. Mix the kale and chickpeas around with a wooden spoon halfway through and leave the feta as it is, but do keep an eye on it towards the end of cooking time so it doesn't go from nice and crisp to burned. Add the pumpkin seeds during the last 5 minutes of cooking, when the kale has just started to crisp and become an intense green-brown.

4. Meanwhile, in a small serving bowl, whisk together the tahini, extra-virgin olive oil, juice of 2 lemons and salt and pepper, adjusting the seasoning to taste. Remove the tray and squeeze the rest of the lemon juice on the greens and chickpeas. Divide between plates and serve with the dressing on the side.

See photo overleaf

MOZZARELLA-TOPPED CHICKEN CUTLETS

Serves 2, 4 for sharing
Prep 5 minutes
Total 20 minutes

---

300 g (10½ oz/2 cups) baby plum (grape) tomatoes, halved

1 x 400 g (15 oz) tin cannellini beans, drained and rinsed

2 garlic cloves, grated or minced

1 medium red onion, sliced

1 teaspoon dried red chilli flakes

1 teaspoon dried oregano

2 skinless, boneless chicken breasts sliced in half lengthwise to form 4 thin cutlets (about 450 g/1 lb)

3 tablespoons olive oil

salt and freshly ground black pepper

225 g (8 oz) mozzarella, sliced or torn into bite-sized chunks

15 g (½ oz/½ cup) basil leaves, thinly sliced or roughly torn (or left whole if small)

extra-virgin olive oil, for drizzling

/ For an impromptu salad, toss some of the beans and tomatoes with a couple of handfuls of baby rocket (arugula) and drizzle with extra-virgin olive oil.

Cut the chicken when it's just out of the fridge as it's easier to do when chilled.

While I'm now an avid sharer when going out to eat, there is still one dish that I refuse to share: the spaghetti bolognese from Madeo in LA.

This goes back to when my friend Sydney and I were in LA right after we graduated from Cornell University in New York. We found this restaurant that felt like a secret hideout – a glimpse of Italy in an upscale setting with the Italian owner's Nonna coming in and out of the kitchen. Little did we know that this was no hidden gem; in fact, over the years, I would come to see Leonardo DiCaprio dining there and then sneaking out through the kitchen, same with Stevie Wonder, Don Johnson and so on.

Their bolognese is still one of my favourite dishes to this day. Sydney and I talk about it like some fabulous former lover, sighing and staring off into the distance each time one of us brings it up. We try to go together whenever we are both in town, and we unanimously agree on one thing: this is not a dish to be shared. So no judgement if you don't want to share this dish or any other dish that you love.

This is sort of, kind of, a deconstructed chicken parmigiana, without the breadcrumbs and some other things. And, in true oven-to-table fashion, it comes together on a baking tray (sheet pan) with minimal involvement from you. I love the garlicky smell that wafts from the oven while it's cooking, the creamy white beans and the gooey, melted cheese.

⏱ Season the chicken with salt and pepper, then set aside and prep the other ingredients as the oven heats up. Slice the mozzarella while the chicken is cooking. You'll have a decent amount of downtime, use that to clean the kitchen, set the table and get ready to eat.

Method

1. Preheat the oven to 200°C (400°F/Gas 6). Set two racks in the oven, one in the middle and the other 15 cm (6 in) from the heat source (if your grill (broiler) is inside your oven).

Use any leftover mozzarella in the Cheesy broccoli sando (page 57) or Go-to weeknight pizza (page 24).

2. Toss the tomatoes, beans, garlic, onion, chilli flakes, oregano, chicken, olive oil, and salt and pepper on a baking tray (sheet pan), coating them well and then spreading out evenly.

3. Roast on the middle rack until the chicken is cooked through and the tomatoes are starting to burst, about 10 minutes. The chicken should be opaque on the top – if you see any bits of raw chicken or pink-ish hues, put it back in for 1–2 minutes.

4. Remove from oven and turn on the grill. Stir the ingredients around a little and place a chunk of mozzarella on each piece of chicken, then scatter the rest of the cheese over the other ingredients. Place under the grill until cheese is bubbly and just browned, about 1–3 minutes, depending on the ferocity of your grill. Top with basil, pepper and a drizzle of high-quality extra-virgin olive oil, if desired.

HOW MEATBALLS
GOT THE BETTER OF ME

Everyone has their food weaknesses, and meatballs are one of mine. My love of meatballs took off when I first ate at Little Owl in the West Village, New York. When it opened, I was instantly taken – well, perhaps obsessed is the right word, as I still have Little Owl and Little Owl Host Line in my phone as contacts – and fell in love with the idyllic corner location set with glass windows, the little perch that you climb up to while waiting for your table and the intimate feel of the restaurant. Their meatball sliders are the clincher: sandwiched between mini Parmesan-crusted buns, topped with a few rocket (arugula) leaves and a well-seasoned tomato sauce that inevitably snakes down my hand, as I get lost in eating it. So there's that.

The obsession continued during my food history class at NYU when I decided to track down the origins of spaghetti and meatballs. I spent days on end scouring old New York restaurant menus, Italian cookbooks like Pellegrino Artusi's 1891 *Science in the Kitchen and the Art of Eating Well* and anything else I could find in the library from the late 1800s and early 1900s, trying to find a trace of when it was 'first invented', which I defined as when it was first served as a single dish. Traditionally, in Italy, pasta is the course served before meatballs, so I wondered if this was perhaps an American combo introduced during the era of the red-checkered tablecloths, candlestick holders and chianti bottles as seen in the movie *Lady and the Tramp*. I don't think I actually ever found the answer, and my professor said as much in my final paper. Anyway, I had a blast trying. Reading through old cookbooks and menus made me feel like some of kind of food detective and spending hours in a library is fun for me – yes, I'm a huge nerd and proud of it.

During my food editor days, we were given press passes to the New York Food and Wine Festival, and I was allowed to go to the first year of Meatball Madness (I know). You can only imagine the ridiculous level of excitement and frenetic energy that was coursing through my veins. Press was allowed in an hour earlier to sample the foods before it got too busy. They should not have let me do that. I think I consumed more than 10 different types of meatballs in less than 30 minutes and then began to have hot flashes. Kind of like a kid going crazy at a birthday party and then going into sugar shock.

I made it through the event, feeling like I had been hit by a truck, only to get home, a few hours later, and be miserably sick. I think my body didn't know how to handle my excitement and was not on the same page. While I admittedly have some issues with managing my food cravings, I hope that you'll enjoy these chicken meatballs that are a lighter, weeknight-take on traditional Italian ones.

BAKED CHICKEN AND RICOTTA MEATBALLS

Serves 2, 4 for sharing
Prep 15 minutes
Total 35 minutes
Makes 20 meatballs

---

400 g (14 oz) Tenderstem broccoli (broccolini), rough stems trimmed and thick pieces cut lengthwise

1 organic lemon, ends trimmed and thinly sliced

4 tablespoons olive oil, divided

salt and freshly ground black pepper

½ teaspoon dried red chilli flakes, or more, if desired

1 large egg

2 garlic cloves, grated or minced

180 g (6½ oz/¾ cup) ricotta, drained and lightly salted

15 g (½ oz/½ cup) parsley leaves and fine stems, roughly chopped

30 g (1 oz/¾ cup) panko breadcrumbs

450 g (1 lb) chicken mince (ground chicken), preferably dark meat

juice from 1 lemon

grated Parmesan, for sprinkling (optional)

✏ Panko aka Japanese breadcrumbs have an airier texture than other breadcrumbs.

🗄 Throw any leftover meatballs in a broth with greens at the end for a quick soup.

I like my broccoli charred and crispy, so that's where this recipe takes you. It is important to make the meatballs uniform, round and slightly smaller than golf balls so that they cook evenly. Even if they're not perfect, they will still taste delicious, and, as we all hopefully know, looks don't really matter.

⏱ Prep the broccoli and lemon, then set up the ingredients for the meatballs.

Method

1. Preheat the oven to 220°C (425°F/Gas 8) with a rack in the middle of the oven.

2. On a baking tray (sheet pan), toss the broccoli and lemon slices with 3 tablespoons of the olive oil, salt, pepper and chilli flakes. Spread evenly on the baking tray and set aside while you make the meatballs.

3. Beat the egg in a mixing bowl, then add garlic and ricotta with 1 teaspoon of salt, parsley, pepper, the rest of the oil, breadcrumbs and meat, and use your hands to gently combine it (too much mushing will make them tough and dry). You should still see pieces of the meat through the seasonings. Lightly wet your hands with water or oil and roll the meat into twenty loose – not tightly packed – rounds, slightly smaller than golf balls, using a gentle rolling motion between your hands (the water is important otherwise they will stick to your hands). Set on large pieces of baking parchment on the counter to make for an easier clean up.

4. Nestle the meatballs in between the broccoli and lemon. Bake until the meatballs are browned and cooked through and the broccoli is crispy, about 15–20 minutes, shaking the baking tray to move the meatballs and turning the tray around halfway to ensure even cooking. Use this time to clean up and set the table. Have a glass of wine if this stressed you out in anyway at all.

5. Remove from the oven, squeeze lemon juice on top, divide between plates, making sure to eat the lemon rinds too, and finish with grated Parmesan, if using.

SLEEVELESS SWEET POTATO JACKETS WITH DIJONNAISE

Serves 2, 4 for sharing
Prep 5 minutes
Total 35 minutes

---

4 small to medium sweet potatoes (try to get even sized ones, if possible), scrubbed and cut in half lengthwise

1 x 400 g (15 oz) tin black beans, drained and rinsed

3 tablespoons olive oil

salt and freshly ground black pepper

2 teaspoons ground cumin

½ teaspoon cayenne pepper

60 g (2 oz/½ cup) pumpkin seeds

2 teaspoons honey

2 teaspoons grated horseradish from a jar, drained of any liquid

2 tablespoons mayonnaise, preferably Kewpie (page 165)

2 tablespoons Dijon mustard

1 ripe Hass avocado, halved, destoned, peeled and sliced, for serving

1 lime, ½ for juice and ½ for serving

Pickled red onions (page 54)

125 g (4 oz/2 cups) baby rocket (arugula)

The Dijonnaise works well as a dipping sauce for meaty fish such as swordfish, with baked sweet potato fries doused with loads of cumin, and lathered on salmon burgers or vegetarian sandwiches.

Some of my most embarrassing memories and stories come from quests for food. Like the time I made my friends bike nearly 10 miles on Nantucket, MA so that I could get a turkey sandwich with Dijonnaise (side note: thank you to my friends and family, I'm not sure why you stick around when I act like this, but I appreciate it very much). The slightly spicy mustard paired with the heat of the horseradish and the silkiness of the mayo was the equivalent of adding chocolate to s'mores. You wonder why anyone would eat it without it. Rather than have you make a turkey sandwich with this (which you should totally do anyway), I paired it with sweet potatoes.

Bake the sweet potatoes, then make the Pickled red onions, the dressing and prep the toppings. Use the rest of the time to clean up or watch a quick show, and dinner will be waiting for you after.

Method

1. Preheat the oven to 200°C (400°F/Gas 6) with a rack in the middle.

2. On a baking tray (sheet pan), rub the sweet potatoes and black beans with the olive oil, salt, pepper, cumin and cayenne. Place the sweet potatoes cut-side down and spread the beans evenly around them.

3. Place in the oven, stirring the beans halfway and turning the baking tray around, until the potatoes can easily be pierced through with a knife and the beans are crunchy, about 30 minutes (larger ones might take longer). During the last 5 minutes, toss the pumpkin seeds onto the baking tray.

4. Meanwhile, in a serving bowl, combine the honey, horseradish, mayonnaise and mustard, mixing until you reach a smooth consistency. Season with salt and pepper. On a cutting board, slice the avocado, squeeze half the lime over it along with a sprinkling of salt. Place the rocket and pickled red onions next to it.

5. When the sweet potatoes are done, it's time for assembly. Top with the bean/seed mixture, rocket, avocado slices and pickled red onions, then drizzle with Dijonnaise and serve with extra lime.

20-MINUTE SPICY SAUSAGE

WITH CRISPY TENDERSTEM BROCCOLI

Serves 2, 4 for sharing
Prep 5 minutes
Total 25 minutes

---

400 g (14 oz) Tenderstem broccoli (broccolini), rough stems trimmed and thick pieces cut lengthwise

1 medium hot red chilli, like a fresno, sliced into coins (optional)

1 teaspoon ground cumin

¼ teaspoon dried red chilli flakes

salt and freshly ground black pepper

3 tablespoons olive oil

450 g (1 lb) spicy sausage (pork, turkey, chicken or beef), casings removed

juice of 1 lemon

grated Parmesan, for sprinkling

15 g (½ oz/½ cup) fresh parsley or coriander (cilantro) leaves and fine stems, roughly torn, for sprinkling

---

I highly recommend finding a sausage source, be it chicken, beef or turkey, that you like and keeping some around. It's great for meals like this, with scrambled eggs for breakfast or last-minute dinners and in soups.

On really lazy nights, rather than cooking this in a frying pan, which you can do, I use this baking method: while cooking, I'll tidy up the kitchen, take a shower (if it's post yoga), shake the pan around while wearing my towel and then put on cosy clothes. Dinner is ready by the time I am, and it feels like a little gift from the cooking gods. Minimal work, maximum happiness.

My sister, a chef, who cooks a lot for professional athletes, told me that she often makes turkey bacon for them as a lean and delicious source of protein – I translated that into meaning all turkey products, such as sausage, are good for you. Do as you will with that information.

Preheat the oven, do the prep then set up while it cooks. Use the cooking time to do your own efficiency moves, be it cleaning the kitchen, setting the table or drinking a glass of wine. All are acceptable.

Method

1. Preheat the oven to 200°C (400°F/Gas 6) with the rack in the middle.

2. On a baking tray (sheet pan), mix together the broccoli, chilli (if using), cumin, chilli flakes, salt, pepper and olive oil until evenly coated. Add the sausage, pulling it apart with your hands into 5 cm (2 in) chunks, a little smaller than golf balls, and distributing them around the baking tray.

3. Bake until the sausage is browned all over and the broccoli is crispy, shaking the tray vigorously halfway through so that everything rolls about a little (or use a wooden spoon to do this). Turn the baking tray around in the oven so that it cooks evenly – about 18–20 minutes total (this is for super crispy broccoli). Test one of the sausage pieces as you get close to the end.

4. Remove the tray from the oven, squeeze lemon juice over it, taste and adjust seasoning as needed, and add a generous sprinkling of cheese. Top with herbs and serve.

FASTER
THAN
DELIVERY

Baked chilaquiles (page 53)

SHORT-CUT
COOKERY

The word 'lazy' has a bad rap. Yet, it's one that I'm fairly often called, though it doesn't seem to be quite the right word to describe me. I typically hear, 'you're lazy, but you're not at the same time.' For example, one of my squash coaches (yes, go ahead and make fun of me: I played squash) once remarked that, while I had a tremendous amount of racquet skill, I was incredibly lazy and had found a way to basically stand still and hit good shots rather than run. This is not a winning strategy for becoming a champion athlete (I didn't make it that far in my squash career), but it does show that there is always a way to minimise energy spent by using skilled short cuts. I would say that this pretty much sums up my approach to cooking. If I can find an easier way to do it and get relatively the same delicious results, well, then I'm going to do that. And I'm definitely going to cut out any fussy bits. The trick is to learn how to maximise taste while minimising time.

In terms of food, this equates to using flavour-packed condiments such as miso pastes, curry pastes, soy sauce, mustard, etc., that do the heavy-lifting for you. Instead of grinding your own fresh curry paste with chillies and spice (which of course is a wonderful thing to do if you have the time and energy) you can buy one that you like, scoop some into the pot, and save yourself the 20 minutes you would have spent making it and cleaning up after, not including the time it took to buy the ingredients. The idea is to have these condiments do the work for you so that you can add a few fresh vegetables and/or high-quality meats/fish and have a fantastic meal on your hands in a short amount of time. Some of these feel like surprisingly fancy dishes considering how quickly they come together, and others are warming and deeply satisfying in how they look and taste.

And, if you want to say f*** it and order in, there's no judgement in that either, because sometimes that's just what needs to be done. On the other nights, whether you're feeling spritely, energetic or on the other side of the spectrum, then I hope these recipes help you out.

WEEKNIGHT CURRY

Serves 2
Prep 10 minutes
Total 20 minutes

---

200 g (7 oz) dried rice noodles

2 tablespoons rapeseed (canola) oil or olive oil

1 shallot, thinly sliced

2 garlic cloves, grated or minced

1 teaspoon grated or minced fresh ginger, from a 5 cm (2 in) piece

1 Thai bird's eye chilli, or small hot red chilli, seeded and diced (use as much as you can handle)

2 tablespoons red or green curry paste

400 ml (13.5 fl oz) tin light coconut milk

8 large peeled prawns (shrimp), deveined

200 g (7 oz/2 cups) mangetout (snow peas), ends trimmed

salt

1 tablespoon fish sauce

15 g (½ oz/½ cup) fresh coriander (cilantro) leaves and fine stems roughly chopped, for sprinkling

45 g (1¾ oz/½ cup) bean sprouts, for sprinkling

lime wedges, for serving

1 small hot red or jalapeño chilli, sliced into coins, for serving (optional)

Swap in mushrooms, baby sweetcorn or other quick-cooking vegetables. Shred leftover chicken and add at the end to warm up. Try white fish instead of prawns (shrimp). Add it at the same time as you would the prawns. You can also skip the noodles and serve with steamed rice.

Curry pastes are true gifts for weeknight cooks as they make a delicious base for dishes, cutting out most of the work. Here, garlic, Thai bird's eye chilli and ginger amplify what's already found in the paste to add a bit more oomph to the overall dish.

Make the recipe a few times, then you'll get the hang of what you like and, from there, throw in whatever quick-cooking vegetables are camping out in your fridge. Try some of the suggestions below.

Boil water for the noodles in a kettle. Prep all of the ingredients as the cooking part moves quickly, and submerge the noodles while you prep so that they are ready in time.

Method

1. Submerge the rice noodles in a shallow bowl of boiling water for 10 minutes until pliable and soft. Drain.

2. Heat the oil in a large frying pan (skillet) over a medium-high heat until shimmering. Add the shallot and cook until softened, about 2 minutes. Add the garlic, ginger and chilli and cook, stirring constantly, until fragrant, about 30 seconds. Mix in the curry paste, stirring to coat the other ingredients, until you smell the spices wafting up, about 1 minute. Stir in a little bit of the coconut milk to deglaze the pan, using a wooden spoon to scrape up any bits on the bottom, then add the remaining milk, stirring to combine. Raise and then adjust the heat to maintain an active simmer.

3. Add the prawns, mangetout and a little salt, cooking until the prawns are pink all over and no longer translucent and the mangetout are crisp tender, about 3–4 minutes. Stir in the fish sauce and drained noodles, coating them with the sauce. Off the heat, top with coriander and bean sprouts. Divide between shallow bowls and serve immediately with lime wedges and sliced chillies, if desired.

HARISSA CHICKPEAS

WITH EGGS AND SPINACH

Serves 2, 4 for sharing
Prep None, unless you count opening the chickpeas
Total 10 minutes

---

2 tablespoons olive oil

2 teaspoons ground cumin

2 teaspoons ground turmeric

2–3 teaspoons harissa, or more, depending on your heat preference

2 x 400 g (15 oz) tins chickpeas (garbanzo beans), drained and rinsed

salt and freshly ground black pepper

125 g (4 oz/2 cups) baby spinach

6 eggs

juice of 1 lemon

low-fat skyr or Greek yoghurt, for serving

Sometimes I mix feta in with the eggs or, if I have leftover Spanish chorizo or sausage, I cook it after adding the harissa, until it's browned/there's no pink, and then continue with the recipe as written.

This dish tastes even better the next day and can be thrown on a bed of raw spinach mixed with quinoa, or just eaten cold for breakfast or a snack.

This is my maybe-I-had-too-much-to-drink-last-night breakfast dish, or for nights when I'm craving something warm and super easy. The spices and harissa paste are what makes this quick scramble of chickpeas, spinach and eggs taste way more exciting than you would think. And topping it with a little yoghurt helps to cool down the heat from the harissa. There's no actual prep work, which is the best part, so you can be in any state while making it.

Method

1. Heat the oil in a 30 cm (12 in) frying pan (skillet) over a medium heat until shimmering. Add the cumin and turmeric until your kitchen smells insanely delicious, about 1 minute. Stir in the harissa and cook until the spices begin tickling your nose, about 15–30 seconds. Add the chickpeas, then season with salt and pepper. Cook until the chickpeas begin to soften, about 2 minutes, then use the back of a wooden spoon to lightly mash a quarter of them, creating a thick paste of sorts.

2. Reduce the heat to medium-low, then stir in the spinach, cooking for about 1 minute so that it lightly wilts, then crack the eggs directly into the pan and stir together using a wooden spoon, breaking up the egg yolks and stirring until it looks like the chickpeas and spinach are swimming in the yellow-tinted egg goo. Season with salt and pepper. Allow to cook, stirring occasionally.

3. When the edges and bottom of the pan start to get darker as the egg sets, gently mix the ingredients around and scrape any egg off the bottom with a wooden spoon, until it sets again. Repeating until the eggs are fluffy and no clear liquid or goo remains, about 2–3 minutes total.

4. Squeeze the lemon juice over the scramble, and check the seasoning one last time, adding salt and pepper if you need to. Top with yoghurt and serve.

BAKED CHILAQUILES

Serves 2, 4 for sharing
Prep 10 minutes
Total 30 minutes

---

150 g (5¼ oz/1 cup) baby plum (grape) tomatoes, quartered

1 corn cob, kernels removed (page 166)

2 spring onions (scallions), white and light green parts, thinly sliced

1 jalapeño or serrano chilli, sliced into thin coins

2 x 175 g (6 oz) Spanish chorizo links, removed from casing and sliced (optional)

1 tablespoon olive oil

salt and freshly ground black pepper

500 ml (17 fl oz/2 cups) passata (strained tomatoes)

½–1 chipotle chilli in adobo, roughly chopped, and 1 teaspoon of the sauce (½ will be pretty hot)

100–125 g (3½ oz/5 cups) unsalted shop-bought tortilla chips or Homemade baked tortilla chips (page 54)

125 g (4 oz/1 cup) crumbly cheese like queso fresco or feta, crumbled

Pickled red onions (page 54)

15 g (½ oz/½ cup) fresh coriander (cilantro) leaves and fine stems, roughly chopped

1 ripe Hass avocado, halved, destoned, peeled and sliced

2–3 limes, cut into wedges, for serving

hot sauce, for serving

Chilaquiles is a wonderful dish, and, in a similar fashion to Panzanella salad (page 122) and Tomato and bread soup (page 81), it's a way to use leftover tortillas, like from the Skirt steak tacos (page 165). I love the softness that the tortillas take on as they soak up the spice-filled sauce. Make the tortilla chips (page 54) before starting the recipe, in the same pan, or, if you don't feel like baking the tortillas yourself, then sub them for unsalted shop-bought chipss.

⏱ Prep the first 4–5 ingredients and then do the rest while they are under the grill (broiler). Use the down time to make the Pickled red onions (page 54), and prep the toppings.

Method

1. Preheat the grill with one rack in the middle and one 15 cm (6 in) from the heat source (if your grill is located inside your oven).

2. On a baking tray (sheet pan) or large ovenproof frying pan (skillet), combine the tomatoes, corn, the whites of the spring onions, chilli and chorizo, if using, with the olive oil, salt and pepper.

3. Place under the grill until the corn is charred, the tomatoes blistered and chorizo browned, about 5–7 minutes, depending on the power of your grill. Remove and preheat the oven to 200°C (400°F/Gas 6).

4. Add the passata, chipotle and sauce to the mixture, using a wooden spoon to combine. Bake for 10–12 minutes so that the passata reduces and the tomato taste cooks off – it might not look like a lot is happening, but if you taste the sauce at increments, you'll notice the difference. Use this cooking time to clean up the kitchen and prep the toppings.

Continued on the next page

Pickled red onions: 1 medium red onion, thinly sliced, red wine vinegar, salt

In a shallow bowl, cover the onion with the vinegar until submerged and a few pinches of salt, stirring to combine. Set aside at room temperature for at least 15 minutes.

Homemade baked tortilla chips: Heat the oven to 200°C (400°F/ Gas 6). Cut 15 cm (6 in) corn tortillas (at least 18 or more) into 4 pieces. On a baking tray (sheet pan), coat them with 3 tablespoons olive oil and a generous amount of salt, so each chip has a light oil sheen. Bake until crispy, about 12–15 minutes, shaking the tray halfway. You can also add a sprinkling of ground cayenne, paprika or cumin to the chips before baking.

Use leftover Pickled red onions for the Skirt steak tacos (page 165) or Sleeveless sweet potato jackets (page 44). They will last up to a week in an airtight container in the fridge.

5. Stir the tortilla chips into the sauce, making sure to coat them thoroughly, then bake in the oven until the chips are soft, about 5 minutes or longer depending on how soft you want them. Remove, then top with the crumbled cheese, pickled red onions, coriander, avocado and reserved greens of the spring onions. Serve with lime wedges and hot sauce, if you like.

MUSHROOMS AND RICOTTA TOAST WITH TONS OF HERBS

Serves 2, 4 for sharing
Prep 5 minutes
Total 20 minutes

---

450 g (1 lb/2 cups) mixed mushrooms, woody stems trimmed, sliced thinly or quartered

250 g (9 oz/1 cup) ricotta, drained and lightly salted

4 pieces crusty bread, toasted

salt and freshly ground black pepper

2 teaspoons ghee

1 tablespoon chives or spring onions (scallions), white and light green parts only, chopped

juice of 1 lemon

15 g (½ oz/½ cup) chopped herbs, such as parsley, mint or basil leaves and fine stems, roughly chopped, for sprinkling

75 g (2½ oz/½ cup) grated Parmesan, or more as desired, for sprinkling

½ teaspoon dried red chilli flakes, for sprinkling (optional)

You can use your favourite mushrooms instead of a mix, just make sure to cut off any woody stems. This is usually the end part, and it will have an unpleasant texture when cooked. Shiitakes are the exception where the entire stem needs to be removed – others can do with just a trim.

You can also use the mushrooms cooked this way as a side dish for anything from roast chicken to pasta.

Does this sound so simple that you're wondering why you bothered buying this book? Well, sometimes we all get stuck in a rut, have a few random things in the fridge or need a little inspo to make a recipe our own. I hope this serves as one of those for you.

I love making this dish when I have loads of fresh herbs and feel a pang of guilt when I open the fridge because I need to use them before they go bad. Dress up this recipe by topping it with a fried egg or soft scrambled eggs with lots of black pepper.

Use a damp paper towel to lightly rub dirt off mushrooms, if needed (don't wash them as they will absorb the water). Toast the bread and prep the herbs while the mushrooms cook.

Method

1. Heat a large cast-iron or non-stick frying pan (skillet) over a medium-high heat until a little smoke comes out of it; kind of like genie smoke coming out of the bottle (a test is to add a drop of water, and it will sizzle when hot). Add the mushrooms to the dry pan and let them cook, untouched for 1 minute, as they release water, shrink and brown, then stir. I know it can feel torturous and tempting not to move them around as you'll hear them sizzle, but try to wait at least 1 minute between each stir, until they've all shrunken in size and are a golden brown, about 5–6 minutes.

2. Meanwhile, spread the ricotta on the toast, and season with salt and pepper.

3. Remove the mushrooms from the heat and stir in the ghee, chives and lemon juice. Divide between the toasts, top with the herbs, Parmesan and dried dried red chilli flakes, if using. Serve any leftover mushrooms on the side.

Photo overleaf

CHEESY BROCCOLI SANDO

Makes 2, 4 for sharing
Prep 5 minutes
Total 10 minutes

---

2 tablespoons olive oil

400 g (14 oz) Tenderstem broccoli (broccolini), rough stems trimmed and thick pieces cut lengthwise

salt and freshly ground black pepper

½ teaspoon dried red chilli flakes, plus more if desired

juice of ½ lemon or more, to taste

225 g (8 oz) mozzarella, sliced into 1 cm (½ in) pieces

1 baguette, cut half widthwise and then partially opened, or 2 mini baguettes and flattened or similar thick bread, toasted

extra-virgin olive oil, for drizzling

/ The better the bread and mozzarella you use, the better this will be. Sometimes, I just make this for myself and then eat the rest of the Tenderstem broccoli (broccolini) as a salad. You could also finish under the grill (broiler) to melt the cheese.

Collegetown Bagels (CTB), a bagel/deli/café/perfect place that was a few steps from the apartment my friends and I lived in, is a Cornell University icon. They served bagels and sandwiches with fun names, some after current Cornell hockey players. I got it in my head that if I ordered the same sandwich everyday, eventually I would win them over and they'd name one after me (this is totally ignoring the fact that I was in no way famous and did not offer a significant contribution to Cornell at that time).

I woke up hungover one morning and craved a mozzarella, tomato, avocado and basil sandwich on toasted ciabatta, so I began ordering that every day. I stuck with it for maybe three or four months, until the end of the academic year, but alas, my dream did not come true.

While I would love to publish that recipe, there's technically no cooking involved, so I substituted the one below, which is something I throw together with leftover vegetables and cheese and use as an excuse to buy a fresh baguette. You should still definitely make The Yaz – the working name for my sandwich – it's just like it sounds. And please send good vibes that CTB will put me up on that board.

Method

1. Heat the oil in a 30 cm (12 in) frying pan (skillet) over a medium-high heat until shimmering. Add the broccoli, salt, pepper and chilli flakes, stirring occasionally, until it is lightly charred and any stems are crisp tender, about 4 minutes. Squeeze the lemon juice over it.

2. Divide the broccoli between the bread pieces, top with mozzarella, a pinch of salt, some pepper and a drizzle of high-quality extra-virgin olive oil.

Photo overleaf

QUICKIE COCONUT MUSSELS

Serves 2, 4 for sharing
Prep 15 minutes (with debearding)
Total 20 minutes

2 tablespoons olive oil

4 spring onions (scallions), white and
light green parts only, separated

1 jalapeño or Thai chilli (or small, hot
green chilli), seeded and minced

salt

2 garlic cloves, grated or minced

1 teaspoon fresh ginger, grated or
minced, from a 5 cm (2 in) piece

1 teaspoon green curry paste (optional)

1 x 400 ml (13.5 fl oz) tin light coconut
milk

900 g (2 lb) mussels, debearded
and scrubbed

4 limes, juice of 2, 2 cut into wedges

1 teaspoon low-salt soy sauce

15 g (½ oz/½ cup) fresh coriander
(cilantro) leaves and fine stems,
for sprinkling

toasted crusty bread, for serving

🖊 To debeard mussels, pinch the hairy
bit coming out of the mussel and pull
it towards the hinged end to remove it.
Discard any mussels that remain open
when tapped with fingers.

Mussels are one of those dishes that seem difficult until
you actually make them, which means you should definitely
make them, especially for people who don't cook very
often and won't know better (is that mean to say?). You'll
have this recipe on the table in 20 minutes, hence why it
is great dish to serve to guests as it looks beautiful and is
low maintenance in terms of prep and cooking. It's also a
fabulous date dish, as it provides an activity of sorts (in case
it's early on and you need some distraction). Just show them
my Pac-Man style mussel eating moves and you've already
got a conversation topic right there (page 111).

⏱ This recipe is pretty quick (unless you need to debeard the
mussels, which will take a bit longer), so have the ingredients
prepped, including opening the tin of coconut milk. You can toast
the bread and clean up the cutting board, knives and prep the herbs
while the mussels are cooking.

Method

1. Heat the oil in a 30 cm (12 in) frying pan (skillet) over a medium-
high heat until shimmering. Add the white part of the spring onions,
chilli and salt, stirring frequently, and cook until softened, about
30 seconds. Add the garlic, ginger, curry paste and cook until
fragrant, about 1 minute.

2. Pour in the coconut milk and raise the heat to bring it to an
active boil then quickly lower the heat to maintain an active simmer.
Add the mussels, cover and cook until they open, shaking the pan
occasionally (this always makes me feel like a pro), about 5 minutes.
Discard any unopened ones. Stir in the juice of 2 limes, soy sauce and
season to taste with salt. Garnish with the green spring onion parts,
coriander leaves and serve with toasted bread and the lime wedges.

FASTER THAN DELIVERY

MUSTARD-TARRAGON CHICKEN THIGHS WITH CAULIFLOWER

Serves 2, 4 for sharing
Prep 10 minutes
Total 30 minutes

---

3 tablespoons olive oil, divided

450 g (1 lb) skinless, boneless chicken thighs, cut into 5 cm (2 in) cubes

salt and freshly ground black pepper

1 small cauliflower (350 g/12 oz), cut into tiny florets (about 2 cups)

½ teaspoon paprika

1 small shallot, minced

1 packed tablespoon chopped tarragon, plus extra for sprinkling (2–3 sprigs)

60 ml (2 fl oz/¼ cup) white wine

200 ml (7 fl oz/¾ cup) low-salt chicken stock (broth)

2 tablespoons Dijon mustard

juice of 1 lemon

crusty bread, to serve

---

*You can use extra stock instead of wine, but it's a great way to use leftover wine that is too far gone to drink.

The cauliflower needs to be cut into tiny trees with most of the stem cut off so it cooks quickly. They should look like trunkless tree tops.

Pan sauces can seem a intimidating (aka sauces made with the brown bits left in the pan and some other ingredients). Accurately approximating how much oil is left in a pan and when liquid is reduced can feel tough to do. For your first few or 100 times, follow the timing instructions and pay attention to how it looks and the visual cues provided. I promise that you will eventually be able to guestimate how much liquid is left and when it's reduced enough, but, until then, don't stress about it. The longer you cook it, the thicker it will get, and, if it gets too thick, then just add a little more liquid at a time. It's fixable.

Cube chicken and season with salt and pepper (meat is always a little easier to cut right out of the fridge as it is a bit firmer). Cut the cauliflower, shallot and tarragon and begin. You can measure out the other ingredients while the chicken and cauliflower are cooking.

Method

1. Heat 2 tablespoons of the oil in a 30 cm (12 in) frying pan (skillet) over a medium heat until shimmering. Season the chicken well with salt and pepper. Add to the pan, stirring occasionally, until the outside is opaque and no pink is visible, about 4–5 minutes. Mix in the cauliflower, season with salt, pepper and paprika, cooking until the chicken is cooked through with a nice browned exterior, or reaches 75°C (165°F), and the cauliflower is crispy and charred, about 12 minutes more. Transfer into a bowl.

2. In the same pan without wiping it out, add the last tablespoon of oil. Add the shallot, tarragon and salt, cooking until it softens, about 1–2 minutes. Pour in the wine, scraping the bottom of the pan to release the crispy, browned bits. Raise the heat to medium-high to reduce the wine until it's just starting to look dry and making you feel nervous, about 2–3 minutes. Add chicken stock to the pan, maintaining an active simmer until the liquid reduces to about 100 ml (⅓ cup), you can roughly eyeball this, about 5 minutes. Stir in the Dijon and adjust seasoning to taste. Add the chicken and cauliflower back in to warm up, coating them with the sauce. Remove from the heat and mix in the lemon juice. Divide the chicken and cauliflower between plates, pour remaining sauce on them, along with the remaining tarragon, pepper and serve with the crusty bread.

BRIGHT DISHES FOR COLD DAYS

Adult instant ramen soup (page 66)

PLEASE DON'T GIVE ME A
BIG SPOON

I have an obsession with small spoons. I've preferred to eat with the 'small' forks and spoons, aka salad forks and teaspoons, ever since I was little – and this hasn't changed as an adult. I collect demitasse spoons – the ones often used for tea or cappuccinos – and have a drawer full of painted blue-and-white ceramic ones from Beijing, smooth wooden ones from Copenhagen and intricate metal-stamped ones from Paris. Basically, I have a lot of tiny spoons. If you ever come over, then I will happily share them with you, and we can enjoy toast soldiers and soft-boiled eggs, which are perfectly suited for my miniature spoons.

In the same vein, I love bowls and prefer eating out of them over plates. There's something so comforting about cradling your hands around a warm bowl of soup, whether it's curling up on the sofa under a blanket on a cold day or twirling a fork in a steaming bowl of noodles, feeling the heat droplets rise up and tickle my face. It also feels way more fun than a plate. There's something intimate and innately nourishing about sipping broth from a bowl, whether it's in the traditional manner of enjoying miso soup or an overfilled bowl that must be slurped down before you can get to the rest, preferably with a small spoon.

Soups might be the original one-pot cooking dishes, where you throw a bunch of ingredients in a pot, either cooking them first and then adding liquid, vice versa or a mixture of both, and that is part of what makes this chapter so wonderful. The Tomato and bread soup (page 81) might feel basic in that it has such few ingredients, but the simplicity of it is what makes it so attractive – it's also great if you're on a budget. The Miso-ginger soup with soba noodles (page 76) is full of delicious and good-for-you ingredients and comes together quickly, plus, it can be scaled down to one for an impromptu meal. Others, like Chicken soup for sick days (page 69), are best made in a large batch, stored in the freezer and meant to be a lifeline on days or nights when you're tired and need something to make you feel better. It's the soup my mother always makes me when I feel sick, so I know nostalgia plays a large part in my love for it, but I don't doubt that you'll also love the bright, lemony taste, loads of fresh herbs and light spice from black pepper. It's guaranteed to perk you up. Here's to staying warm and with a full belly, wherever in the world you are.

ADULT INSTANT RAMEN SOUP

Serves 2
Prep 5 minutes
Total 20 minutes

2 x 90 g (3 oz) ramen noodle nests (discard any flavour packets)

1 tablesooon sesame oil, for coating noodles

1½ tablespoons ghee

2 spring onions (scallions), white and light green parts only, thinly sliced

2 teaspoons or up to 1 tablespoon sambal oelek or other chilli sauce, depending on desired heat level

450 g (1 lb) pork mince (ground pork)

salt

1 litre (34 fl oz/4 cups) low-salt chicken or beef stock (broth)

3 tablespoons mirin (see note below)

50 ml (1¾ fl oz/¼ cup) low-salt soy sauce

2 tablespoons miso paste

2 tablespoons wakame

Mirin is a sweet Japanese rice wine. If you don't think that you'll use it again or aren't ready for that level of commitment, then use 3 tablespoons white wine or sherry with ½–1 tablespoon sugar mixed in. You can also substitute ghee for butter or a neutral oil.

Use leftover wakame in the Miso-ginger soup with leafy greens (page 76).

When I was a kid, my mother was convinced that she could make miso soup at home after we became obsessed with eating it out (bless her). She went through countless unsuccessful attempts, then came the eureka moment: 'you add the miso at the end!' I don't know where she learned that essential trick, but it made all the difference.

Before we go any further, I would like to clarify that this is by no means a traditional ramen recipe. See how I'm trying to avoid getting shouted at by the internet? While it is completely worth the effort, it's not something that makes sense for the purposes of this book. I much prefer to leave that to the ramen experts; however, I do get an immense amount of joy from slurping noodles (ramen etiquette includes quickly eating the noodles and slurping – how awesome is that?), so I created this ramen-like noodle soup that can be made at home in just about 20 minutes.

There's minimal prep to this recipe so first boil the water. While it reaches a boil, cut the spring onions (scallions) and measure out the ingredients and set up the toppings during this time or when the pork is cooking.

Method

1. Half-fill a flameproof casserole dish (Dutch oven) with water and bring to a vigorous boil. Cook the noodles according to the package directions until just tender, about 2 minutes, then drain into a colander in the sink and immediately drizzle with sesame oil, using a fork and spoon to toss and coat the noodles until they have a glossy sheen so that they don't stick together. Leave in the sink (just be careful if you decide to wash something else).

2. Heat 1 tablespoon of the ghee in the same pan over a medium heat until melted. Add the white part of the spring onions, sambal and pork and season well with salt, breaking the pork apart into tiny, crumb-sized pieces with a wooden spoon. Let the pork it sit and make contact with the pan, stirring occasionally, until the pork is browned and cooked through, about 4–5 minutes.

Optional Toppings

Enoki mushrooms: add them with the miso and wakame as they will soften and cook in the same amount of time.

Dried nori: this will add a textural crunch, especially if you toast it lightly before and then cut into strips using kitchen scissors.

Soft-boiled egg: yes, you would have to make these in another pan, but a peeled and halved 6-minute egg – one that has been in boiling water for exactly that length of time, then put in an ice bath or run under cold water to stop the cooking process – would add a layer of creaminess to it.

Furikake or sesame seeds: finish with black sesame seeds from the Miso-ghee chicken thighs with roasted radishes (page 29) (white ones work, too).

Kimchi: great for gut bacteria, it can be served on the side or on top at the end.

Spinach: stir in some baby or chopped spinach at the end, for more green.

3. Add the stock, raise the heat to reach a boil, then adjust to maintain a gentle simmer. Stir in the mirin, soy, miso paste and wakame, stirring occasionally. Cook until the miso dissolves and the wakame is soft and silky, about 4 minutes. Pour in the noodles, swirling them around with a wooden spoon to mix them in, then remove from the heat and adjust seasoning as needed with salt or more heat. Stir in the last bit of ghee, if desired, then divide between bowls and finish with toppings of your choice.

TOMATO-POACHED COD
WITH FRESH HERBS

Serves 4
Prep 5 minutes
Total 25 minutes

---

2 tablespoons olive oil

1 shallot, thinly sliced

salt and freshly ground black pepper

1 garlic clove, thinly sliced

½ teaspoon dried dried red chilli flakes
or more, as desired

2 x 400 g (14 oz) tins chopped tomatoes
and their liquid

250 ml (8½ fl oz/1 cup) low-salt
vegetable stock (broth) or water

4 x 150 g (5 oz) cod fillets

30 g (1 oz/1 cup) parsley or basil leaves
and fine stems, roughly chopped or
torn, for sprinkling

toasted crusty bread, for serving

Salting the cod generously on all sides, then setting aside while you prep the other ingredients allows it to keep its shape during the cooking process. Rinse the salt off with cold water and pat dry, then salt and pepper it before adding the sauce.

It's helpful to get similar-sized fillets so that they cook evenly.

Stir in ½–1 tablespoon harissa with shallots when adding garlic to add more heat to the dish.

Back when my sister lived in Paris, I scanned through the Rose Bakery cookbook in her apartment when visiting, which was full of high-quality, minimal and delicious recipes. A variation of their poached cod in tomato water was one I made over and over again, for both myself and guests, even when serving hot foods wasn't necessarily appropriate. I made this for one of my best friends, Matty, in my tiny NYC apartment when we were in our early twenties, in the height of summer – my sad little air-conditioning unit was not much help. His response, in between wiping the sweat off his brow was, 'this is really good, though it does feel hard to eat a hot dish in the summer'. Fair. This is all to say that this recipe is really easy, good for you, and can slip into your weeknight rotation when you want to look fancy and feel good with minimal effort (aka my goal in life).

Method

1. Heat the oil in a wide, shallow frying pan (skillet) over a medium heat until shimmering. Add the shallot and salt, stirring until softened, about 3 minutes. Add the garlic and chilli flakes, stirring until fragrant, about 30 seconds more. Pour in the tomatoes and stock and raise the heat to achieve an active boil. Adjust it to maintain an active simmer, stirring occasionally, and season with salt and pepper. Let it cook for about 10 minutes so that the tomatoes lose their tinned taste and the liquid reduces slightly.

2. Season the fish with salt and pepper and add to the sauce, adjusting the heat to maintain a gentle active simmer. Cook until the fish is opaque and easily flakes when touched, about 5 minutes, spooning the sauce over the fillets. If they are not fully submerged then turn them over halfway. (Thick fillets will take a little longer.) Toast the bread.

3. Divide the fish between serving bowls and spoon the tomato sauce over. Finish with pepper and parsley and serve with the bread for dipping.

Photo on pages 70–71

CHICKEN SOUP

FOR SICK DAYS

Serves 2, 4 for sharing
Prep 10 minutes
Total 50 minutes

---

2 tablespoons olive oil

2 small carrots, diced

2 celery stalks, diced

1 medium red onion, diced

3 medium yellow potatoes, diced into
  1 cm (½ in) pieces

salt and freshly ground black pepper

1 x 900 g (2 lb) whole Cornish hen or
  small chicken

2 tablespoons tomato purée (paste)

1.5 litres (51 fl oz/6 cups) water

4 angel or rice vermicelli noodle nests

60 g (1 bunch/2 cups) fresh coriander
  (cilantro), leaves and fine stems
  roughly chopped

juice of 2 lemons

✏ You can freeze the chicken bones
to make another chicken stock later.

▮ Make sure to stir in some fresh
lemon juice and coriander after you
reheat the leftover soup.

The best part of this soup – and kind of a genius move on my mother's part – is that it naturally creates a built-in chicken stock, which is one of many reasons why it's important to buy the best quality chicken you can. This aspect, paired with the bright taste from the lemon and coriander, is what makes it so great as it feels filling and light at the same time. And, as I am fond of saying, it's easy, peasy, lemon squeezy.

Method

1. Heat the oil in a flameproof casserole dish (Dutch oven) large enough to fit the chicken and water over a medium-high heat until shimmering. Add the carrots, celery, onion, potatoes and a generous amount of salt (I suggest, circling the pot once while letting salt stream down from your fingertips), stirring frequently, until the onions have softened and become more translucent, about 3 minutes (the carrots should become brighter). Meanwhile, generously season the chicken with salt and pepper.

2. Use a wooden spoon to push the ingredients around the sides of the pan, then place the chicken breast side down, cooking until it easily releases from the pan and the skin has started to brown, around 5 minutes. Flip, then mix in the tomato purée, stirring with the other ingredients and allowing the other side to cook, about 1–2 minutes more. Add the water, raising the heat to a boil and then adjusting it to maintain an active simmer. Cook, stirring every few minutes, to make sure nothing is sticking, seasoning as needed, until the chicken is cooked through, about 15–20 minutes or until it reaches 75°C (165°F) when pierced through the thigh away from the bone (if your little chickie is bobbing up out of the water, then turn it over halfway). Remove the chicken and set aside in a bowl.

3. Keep the soup at a gentle simmer and use a fork and knife (or your hands once it's cooled a bit) to shred the chicken. Discard the skin and bones, stir the chicken and any juices back into the pot. Add the noodles, and season with salt and pepper.

4. When the noodles have softened and the chicken is warmed through, about 3 minutes more, remove from the heat, then squeeze in the lemon juice and stir in the coriander. Adjust the seasoning and lemon juice as needed. Finish with a generous amount of pepper and ladle into serving bowls.

30-MINUTE GREEN CHICKEN CHILI

Serves 2, 4 for sharing
Prep 15 minutes
Total 30 minutes

---

2 tablespoons olive oil, divided

1 medium yellow onion, diced

2 jalapeño chillis, 1 seeded and diced,
  1 sliced for sprinkling

2 poblano or green (bell) peppers,
  seeded and diced

1 tin tomatillos, drained or 6 fresh
  husked or 6 fresh green tomatoes,
  roughly chopped

salt and freshly ground black pepper

2 garlic cloves, grated or minced

1 tablespoon ground cumin

1 tablespoon dried oregano

450 g (1 lb) skinless, boneless
  chicken thighs

500 ml (17 fl oz/2 cups) low-salt
  chicken stock (broth)

125 g (4 oz) tin mild or hot chopped
  green chillies, preferably Hatch

2 limes, juice of 1, 1 sliced into wedges,
  for serving

15 g (½ oz/½ cup) fresh coriander
  (cilantro), fine stems and leaves
  roughly chopped

1 Hass avocado, halved, destoned,
  peeled and sliced, for
  serving (optional)

/ You can add white beans when you
add the chicken. Then, use the back of a
wooden spoon to mash the beans against
the side of the pan to thicken it.

While working at *Food & Wine* magazine in my early twenties, some of the editors were raving about Hatch green chillies as we chatted, and, not wanting to seem like a total idiot, I nodded enthusiastically and then immediately went to search what these things were. They are, in fact, pretty awesome, and come from a town called Hatch in New Mexico, USA. You can add them to soups, stews, salsas or use as toppings for burgers or pizzas for a great depth of flavour. They range in heat level (and also offer a subtle sweetness to them), so buy whichever are better for your palate.

This recipe is in no way meant to replicate a traditional chili verde (from New Mexico) but, regardless, it is pretty good. It's one of those dishes you'll make and be like, whoa, that's a lot better than I expected in this short amount of time. You may have to do a bit searching for fresh tomatillos if they're not readily available, but the tinned variety will always be available online and in specialty stores.

Method

1. Heat the oil in a large flameproof casserole dish (Dutch oven) over a medium heat until shimmering. Add the onion, jalapeño, peppers, tomatillos, salt and pepper, stirring frequently, until softened, about 5 minutes. Add the garlic, spices and cook, stirring constantly, until fragrant, about 1 minute.

2. Season the chicken with salt and pepper, then add to the pan. Pour in the chicken stock and raise the heat to maintain a gentle simmer (avoid bringing to a boil). Cook until the chicken is cooked through, about 10 minutes. If the chicken pieces are not completely submerged, then turn them over halfway. Remove the chicken and place on a plate or in a shallow bowl. Use a fork and knife to shred the chicken, then add it back along with any liquid and the green chillies. Cook until the chicken is warmed through, about 2 minutes; squeeze in the lime and adjust seasoning as needed. Ladle into bowls and top with coriander, avocado (if using) and sliced jalapeño. Serve with lime wedges.

A VEGETARIAN, NOT-SO-TEXAS, CHILI

WITH BLACK BEANS AND SQUASH

Serves 4
Prep 10 minutes
Total 30 minutes

2 tablespoons olive oil

1 small butternut squash (450 g/1 lb), peeled and cubed (page 16)

salt and freshly ground black pepper

1 large onion, diced

1 yellow and 1 orange (bell) pepper, seeded and diced

1 tablespoon ground cumin

1 teaspoon dried oregano

2 garlic cloves, grated or minced

3 chipotle chillies in adobo, roughly chopped, and 1 tablespoon of the sauce, for a spicy chilli, but reduce for less heat

500 ml (17 fl oz/2 cups) low-salt vegetable stock (broth)

2 x 400 g (15 oz) tins black beans, drained and rinsed

4 spring onions (scallions), white and light green parts only, sliced

125 g (4 oz/1 cup) grated Cheddar, for serving

1 ripe Hass avocado, halved, destoned, peeled and diced, for serving

1 small hot red chilli, seeded and diced, for serving

2 limes, cut into wedges, for serving

shop-bought tortilla chips or Homemade baked tortillas chips, for serving (optional) (page 54)

Even though I spent a fair time in Texas growing up on my uncle's ranch, this recipe does not resemble a traditional Texas chili in anyway. In fact, I might even get in trouble with the internet by using the word chili. There's a lot of rules and discussions about what goes into and what constitutes a Texas chili (seriously, search it and you'll see what I mean). So let's say this is ignoring all of that and meant to be a quick and easy weeknight meal that also happens to be meat-free and full of good-for-you ingredients.

Method

1. Heat the oil in a 30 cm (12 in) frying pan (skillet) or flameproof casserole dish (Dutch oven) over a medium-high heat until shimmering. Add the butternut squash and season with salt and pepper. Cook, stirring occasionally, until lightly browned, about 5 minutes. Add the onion, peppers and salt, stirring and cooking until softened, about 3 minutes. Add the cumin, oregano and garlic, cooking until fragrant, about 1 minute.

2. Stir in the chipotle chillies, their sauce, the stock and beans and cook, adjusting the heat to maintain an active simmer, until the squash is tender, about 10 minutes (try a bite). Mash half the beans gently with a wooden spoon against the side of the pan to thicken it, then season with salt and pepper as needed. Ladle into bowls and top with spring onions, grated cheese, avocado and chilli. Serve with lime wedges, tortilla chips, and more cheese because, why not?

To save yourself time and energy, buy pre-cut butternut squash.

You can sub the squash for sweet potato and leave out the chipotle peppers if you don't want heat or want to make it child-friendly.

Freeze leftover chipotle chillies in sauce in plastic food storage bags or airtight containers for future use or make Baked chilaquiles (page 53).

MISO-GINGER SOUP
WITH LEAFY GREENS

Serves 2
Prep 10 minutes
Total 30 minutes

1 tablespoon sesame, neutral or
olive oil

1 shallot, thinly sliced

salt and freshly ground black pepper

1 garlic clove, grated or minced

1 teaspoon fresh ginger, peeled and
minced, from a 5 cm (2 in) piece

1.5 litres (50 fl oz/6 cups) low-salt
vegetable stock (broth) or water

2 tablespoons soy sauce

75 g (2½ oz/1 cup) shiitake mushrooms,
stems removed, caps sliced

150 g (5¼ oz/2 packed cups) chard,
leaves removed from stems, cut into
5 cm (2 in) ribbons

185 g (6½ oz) soba noodles (2 bundles)

2 tablespoons miso paste

2 spring onions (scallions), white and
light green parts only, thinly sliced

45 g (1¾ oz/½ cup) bean sprouts or pea
shoots, for sprinkling

15 g (½ oz/½ cup) fresh herb leaves
such as coriander (cilantro) or mint,
for sprinkling

sesame seeds and/or dried red chilli
flakes, for sprinkling

✏ To make it for one, skip the second
bundle of soba noodles, reduce the
liquid to 1 litre (34 fl oz/4 cups), shiitake
to 30 g (1 oz/⅓ cup), chard to 75 g
(2½ oz/1 cup), and reduce the soy sauce
and miso paste by half as well.

A complaint I often get from friends is that it's hard to cook for one as most recipes are meant for two to four people, and who wants to eat the same thing all week? Well, I've found that the trick, and part of the aim of this book, is to help you figure out how to use ingredients already in your fridge or cupboard to make easy meals for one, two or four people (or even more if you have loads of friends, well done you) as you learn how to make soups, cook scallops, swap greens for one another and use leftover herbs as you like. I often make easy, vegetarian dishes for myself that come together quickly, like this one, which can easily be scaled down to serve one (see recipe note).

⏱ This comes together quickly, and, if you're comfortable with cutting vegetables, you can cut the mushrooms and chard while the stock is simmering (you'll have about 5 minutes).

Method

1. Heat oil in a large flameproof casserole dish (Dutch oven) over a medium heat until shimmering. Add the shallot and a pinch of salt stirring occasionally until soft, about 3 minutes. Add the garlic and ginger, stirring constantly, until fragrant, about 30 seconds. Pour in the stock and soy sauce, raising heat to achieve an active boil, then adjust heat to maintain an active simmer.

2. Simmer for about 5 minutes so the ingredients cook together, then add the mushrooms, greens and noodles, cooking according to the package instructions, or until the noodles are tender but not squishy, and the chard has softened, about 4 minutes. Off the heat, stir in the miso paste and adjust the seasoning as needed. Ladle into bowls and top with spring onions, bean sprouts/herbs and sesame seeds and chilli flakes.

▭ Use leftover wakame from the Adult instant ramen soup (page 66) instead of the chard, or as an addition to and add at the same time.

CURRIED BUTTERNUT SQUASH SOUP WITH KALE AND QUINOA

Serves 4
Prep 10 minutes
Total 30 minutes

2 tablespoons olive oil, divided

1 medium butternut squash (1 kg/2 lb 4 oz), peeled and cut into 5 cm (2 in) cubes (page 16)

1 medium onion, diced

1 medium carrot, peeled and cut into 2.5 cm (1 in) coins

salt and freshly ground black pepper

2 teaspoons curry powder (or more, depending on how strong you like your curry)

1 teaspoon ground cumin

½ teaspoon dried red chilli flakes

150 g (5 oz/¾ cup) quinoa, rinsed

1 litre (34 fl oz/4 cups) low-salt vegetable stock (broth)

200 g (7 oz) curly kale or cavolo nero (lacinato kale) or other leafy greens, leaves removed from stems, cut into 2.5 cm (1 in) ribbons or hand torn (about 2 cups)

juice of 1 lemon

30 g (1 oz/¼ cup) toasted pumpkin seeds (page 16), for sprinkling

15 g (½ oz/½ cup) fresh coriander (cilantro) fine stems and leaves, roughly torn, for sprinkling

1 jalapeño chilli, seeded and thinly sliced, for sprinking (optional)

Butternut squash can be a pain to cut (I always feel like I'm going to lose a finger doing it), so if buying pre-cut squash makes your life easier, then by all means, do it. Or see page 16.

The beginning of this recipe has a lot of action, and you'll find yourself stirring, adding and toasting the quinoa for a nuttier taste, but it's step-by-step and should be easy to do if you have everything within arm's reach (you don't want to be scrambling in the cupboards searching for spices when you start). After that, it's more of a 'leave and check on' situation – a perfect time for refilling your glass of wine, setting the table or calling your mother.

Make, eat and repeat when you want a ton of vegetables on a cold day. Plus, it gets better the next day, and the day after that.

Prep the kale, wash the coriander (cilantro) and toast the pumpkin seeds while the quinoa is cooking. You can use that time to clean up the kitchen as well.

Method

1. Heat the oil in a large flameproof casserole dish (Dutch oven) over medium heat until shimmering. Add the butternut squash, onion and carrot and season with salt and pepper. Cook, stirring occasionally, until squash is lightly browned and softened, about 5 minutes. Stir in the curry powder, cumin and chilli flakes and cook until fragrant, about a minute more. Add the quinoa, stirring to combine, and let it toast, about 1 minute.

2. Add the stock, cover and raise the heat to achieve and maintain an active boil; cook until the quinoa is done and spirals are open, about 9 minutes. Stir in the kale, cooking until wilted, about 2 minutes more. Remove from the heat, season with lemon juice, salt and pepper and divide between serving bowls. Top with pumpkin seeds, coriander leaves and sliced chilli, if using.

THAI LEMONGRASS-COCONUT CHICKEN SOUP

Serves 2
Prep 10 minutes
Total 35 minutes

---

1 tablespoon olive oil

3–4 lemongrass stalks, inner pale parts only, roughly chopped into 2.5 cm (1 in) pieces (page 15)

1 shallot, thinly sliced

1 Thai or serrano chilli (or small hot green chilli), seeded and diced

salt

1 teaspoon fresh ginger, grated or minced, from a 5 cm (2 in) piece

1 garlic clove, grated or minced

450 g (1 lb) boneless, skinless chicken breasts

1 litre (34 fl oz/4 cups) low-salt chicken stock (broth)

400 ml (13.5 fl oz) tin light coconut milk

100 g (3½ oz/2 cups) enoki mushrooms, ends trimmed

50 g (1¾ oz/½ cup) mangetout (snow peas), ends trimmed

50 g (1¾ oz/½ cup) baby sweetcorn (optional)

1 teaspoon green curry paste (optional)

2 tablespoons fish sauce

30 g (1 oz/1 cup) basil or coriander (cilantro) leaves, roughly torn, for sprinkling

4 limes, 2 juiced, 2 cut into wedges

➤ Swap sliced button or chestnut (cremini) mushrooms for enoki.

Once, when interviewing a *Top Chef* contestant in Kalustyan's – a great speciality shop for spices in Manhattan – he whipped out a lemongrass stalk from a basket, cracked it open and held it out for me to smell. The fragrance is both bright, warming and comforting in an intoxicating way – I discovered what an instant flavour bomb lemongrass can be.

A play on Tom Kha Gai, a Thai soup, this recipe is great when you want a lightish feeling soup with minimal effort.

⏱ Use the chicken poaching time to prep the vegetables and measure out remaining ingredients.

Method

1. Heat the oil in a large flameproof casserole dish (Dutch oven) over a medium heat until melted and shimmering. Add the lemongrass, stirring frequently, until the fragrance fills the room (I'm excited for you to experience how good it smells), about 2 minutes. Add the shallot, chilli and season with salt, stirring occasionally until softened, about 3 minutes. Add the ginger and garlic, stirring constantly until fragrant, about 1 minute more.

2. Season the chicken breasts with salt, and add to the pan along with the stock and coconut milk, adjusting the heat to maintain a gentle simmer (try to avoid boiling it, if possible). Poach in the liquid until just cooked through, about 15 minutes or until it reads 75°C (165°F) in the thickest part of the breast (skim off any white scum that's on the surface).

3. Remove the chicken and put into a shallow bowl or plate and, using a fork and knife, shred it, while keeping the liquid at a gentle simmer. Return the chicken and any liquid into the pan, along with the mushrooms, mangetout, baby sweetcorn and curry paste, if using, and fish sauce, stirring occasionally, until the chicken is warmed through and the mushrooms are silky and cooked, about 2 minutes more. Off the heat, stir in the lime juice (discard the lemongrass stalks or remove as you eat). Ladle into serving bowls and garnish with herbs and serve with lime wedges.

SOME LIKE IT HOT

When I was learning how to cook, aka reading and cooking my way through every cookbook I could get my hands on in my early twenties, I decided that I needed to first master tomato sauce. As a kid, I used to eat tomatoes like apples, so this felt like a natural choice.

Over the course of two years, I tried every recipe I could to nail 'my' tomato sauce. I started with one of Jamie Oliver's Italian cookbooks – I studied it religiously, making notes and trying to memorise as much as I could. I remember the first few times I would check every word in the recipe to make sure I was doing it correctly. How long do I stir for again? Do I stir frequently or occasionally? Words thrown about so casually yet they mean so much to the newbie cook. I hadn't yet learned to cook from sight or taste, which, as you will find, are more important than timing and instructions.

I moved through several other chefs, ending up at Scott Conant, chef of Scarpetta, which now has numerous locations across the US. I used to live next door to the first (and now defunct) Scarpetta on the corner of 14th and 9th street in New York and would often see Scott sitting outside in the early afternoons during the warmer months. He'd share a wink or a wave, sometimes paired with small banter, and I'd giggle and try to not be too awkward in my response, and run upstairs and think, 'hehe, he doesn't know that I am currently testing out his tomato sauce recipe'. (Sorry, Scott, I hope that wasn't weird for you. I really do love your restaurant.)

Now, even when I use fresh tomatoes, I'm far too lazy to blanch and peel them (hats off to those of you who do it), and even though it is quite fun to crush them with your hands, I rarely do that either. I also don't mind tomato skins, but I know they are kind of ugly and sometimes they roll up and become hard, so it's a bit like, what is this mini fruit leather look-alike doing here, but then you just push it to the side, and you're good to go. Food doesn't have to be perfect after all, and neither do you (boom, life lesson thrown in there).

The tomato sauce you'll find in this book is the result of all of the years of research, but I do hope that you play around with it and make it your own.

SIDE NOTE

As an overall note, I do like things on the spicy side, especially my tomato sauce, so adjust the heat level to your preference.

TOMATO AND BREAD SOUP
WITH SPINACH

Serves 3–4
Prep 5 minutes
Total 30 minutes

2 tablespoons olive oil

1 shallot, minced

salt and freshly ground black pepper

150 g (5 oz/1 cup) cherry tomatoes, halved or quartered, depending on size

2 garlic cloves, grated or minced

½ teaspoon dried red chilli flakes

2 x 400 g (14 oz) tins chopped tomatoes and their liquid

250 ml (8½ fl oz/1 cup) water

1 Parmesan rind (optional)

300 g (10 oz/2 cups) stale torn bread, preferably a thick rustic-style or baguette, lightly toasted

80 g (3 oz/1½ packed cups) spinach, roughly chopped and thick stems removed

15 g (½ oz/½ cup) basil leaves and fine stems, thinly sliced, for sprinkling

2 tablespoons fresh chives, thinly sliced, for sprinkling (optional)

grated Parmesan, for sprinkling

/ For more umami, either grate some Parmesan directly into the sauce while it's cooking, or add a teaspoon of fish sauce – the fishiness will cook off, I promise.

Toast torn bread cubes with a little olive oil in the oven at 200°C (400°F/ Gas 6) until browned and toasted but not crouton level, about 8 minutes.

Admittedly, it sounds basic. But I feel like being basic isn't that bad all the time. Plus, it's good to have an arsenal of uncomplicated, back-pocket recipes when you have a hankering for something warm and cosy. This recipe is one that I make over and over again as it's relatively inexpensive. *Papa al Pomodoro*, a rustic Italian dish that this is based off is meant, like the Panzanella salad (page 122), to be a way to use up leftover bread that's bordering on, or has gone, stale.

⏱ Cut the shallots and tomatoes, then make the soup and toast the bread during this time, if necessary. Use the downtime to set the table and have some wine. Chop the herbs after you add the bread as they darken quickly once cut, so do them as near the end as possible.

Method

1. Heat the oil in a large flameproof casserole dish (Dutch oven) over a medium heat until shimmering. Add the shallot and a pinch of salt, stirring frequently until just softened, about 2 minutes.

2. Add the fresh tomatoes and season with salt, stirring frequently, until the skins begin to blister and the tomatoes start to break down, about 3 minutes. Add the garlic and chilli flakes, stirring until fragrant but not browned, about 30 seconds more. Add the tinned tomatoes, water and Parmesan rind, if using. Season with salt and pepper. Raise the heat to achieve an active boil across the surface, then reduce the heat to maintain an active simmer, until the liquid thickens, about 15 minutes. Stir occasionally and adjust the seasoning by tasting the sauce and adding a little more salt, pepper and/or chilli flakes.

3. Add the bread and spinach, stirring to combine and submerge the bread pieces. Adjust the seasoning as needed, stirring occasionally. Cook until the bread is soft but not totally falling apart and spinach has wilted, about 5 minutes more.

4. Spoon into bowls and top with basil, chives and a generous grating of cheese.

CURRIED LENTILS
WITH CUCUMBER-GARLIC YOGHURT

Serves 4
Prep 10 minutes
Total 50 minutes

2 tablespoons oil

½ tablespoon ghee (optional)

2 small carrots, peeled and diced

2 celery stalks, diced

1 large red onion, diced

1 jalapeño chilli, seeded and diced

salt and freshly ground black pepper

1 tablespoon curry powder

1 teaspoon ground cumin

2 garlic cloves, grated or minced

200 g (7 oz/1 cup) dried green lentils

400 g (15 oz) tin chickpeas (garbanzo beans), drained and rinsed

750 ml (25 fl oz/3 cups) low-salt chicken or vegetable stock (broth)

185 g (6½ oz/3 cups) baby spinach

250 g (9 oz/1 cup) thick yoghurt, such as Greek or skyr

½ cucumber, peeled and diced or grated

extra-virgin olive oil, for drizzling

juice of 1 lemon

15 g (½ oz/½ cup) fresh mint leaves and fine stems, thinly sliced, for sprinkling

✎ Stir in more spinach if you're reheating it as is or serve it on top of cooked quinoa and more greens for a lunch or dinner salad.

When I was 26, I did yoga teacher training in Northern California. We were surrounded by redwoods, and so high up that, in the mornings, we would be higher than the fog – it looked like we were floating above the clouds. It was a wonderful experience for so many reasons, but one is that it's where I first had *kitchari*, an Ayurvedic dish made of lentils and mung beans with loads of spices. This recipe is my spice-and-lentil-filled ode to that warming dish.

⏱ There is a lot of downtime in this recipe, so make the yoghurt, clean up the kitchen or do something that makes you happy while the lentils are cooking.

Method

1. Heat the oil and ghee, if using, in 30 cm (12 in) frying pan (skillet) over a medium heat until shimmering. Stir in the carrot, celery, onion, chilli and season with salt and pepper. Cook, stirring occasionally, until the onion has softened and the carrot becomes a more vibrant orange colour, about 5 minutes. Mix in the curry powder, cumin and half the garlic, stirring constantly, until fragrant, about 1 minute. Add the lentils, chickpeas and stock, raise the heat to achieve an active boil, then adjust it to maintain a gentle simmer.

2. Cook until the lentils have softened and are tender to the bite, stirring every 5–10 minutes to make sure nothing is sticking to the bottom, about 25–30 minutes total (there should still be a little liquid inthe pan so that they look wet, if not, add 4–8 tablespoons more stock or water). Stir in the spinach, until it begins to wilt, about 2 minutes more.

3. Meanwhile, in a small serving bowl, combine the yoghurt, remaining garlic, cucumber, season with salt and a drizzle of oil until smooth. Adjust the seasoning to taste.

4. Remove the lentils from the heat, stir in the lemon juice, seasoning as needed. Spoon into bowls and top with the yoghurt and mint leaves.

GLUTEN, GRAINS AND GOOD STUFF

Cheesy pasta bake (page 95)

I LIKE TO
DIG

I have this weird thing where I use my index and middle finger to dig out the doughy centre of bread, much like a forklift clearing rubble from the street. If you grew up in my household, then you would most definitely find a hollowed middle in whatever loaf of bread was left unattended in the kitchen.

I still do it to this day, whether it's a fresh baguette from Arcade Bakery in New York or La Fromagerie in London, often without realising that I'm doing it. While I think tearing off a piece of baguette and eating it in the street is one of the best parts of life, I then continue to dig a little tunnel unless someone takes the bread away from me. I also tend to pick up bread and smell it, which gets me odd looks, especially in fancy restaurants.

Why do I do this? I can't say other than that I love the soft, doughy and plump texture – it makes me inexplicably happy. I'm just sorry for my friends and family who have to find hollowed-out loaves whenever I'm with them.

This is all to say that I have a deep love for bread, and it really upsets me that people are so mean to it. My hero during middle/high school, when the Atkins diet was the fad of the moment, was my friend's mother, who would go around to small bakeries both in Boston and NYC to buy bread because she didn't want them to go out of business. Yes, eating too much of anything isn't great for your waistline or how you feel, but

TUNNELS
IN LOAVES OF BREAD

playing the blame game isn't a great idea either. And gluten or carbs aren't always the sole issue for weight gain (let's give a shout-out to processed foods, fast food and lifestyle choices, to name a few).

It's always been important to me to maintain a positive relationship with food, as I never wanted to see it as something to be anxious or guilty about – which I think is difficult today – because it brings so much happiness into my life. For that reason, I've always tried to subscribe to a Marie Kondo-like approach to eating, in terms of finding out what brings me joy in both how I feel during and after I eat (and being honest with myself about this, which is the hard part). Rather than looking at bread as this super-indulgent thing to be fearful of and then feel guilty about after consuming it, I make sure to eat really fantastic and delicious bread and an amount that leaves me satisfied and happy. I eat it with intention, and then don't let myself feel badly about it after.

I think that an approach to food that celebrates it as something that can bring us nourishment and joy is the best relationship to develop and what will really make you feel good in the long run. It's not easy, of course, and takes time to alter your perspective, but I do believe that it will make a difference. So, eat these pastas and other gluten, grain and good-stuff related dishes when you crave them, and enjoy every single bite of it.

And apologies in advance if I ever eat the inside of your bread when you're not looking.

PASTA ALLA GRICIA
WITH KALE

Serves 4
Prep 10 minutes
Total 30 minutes

500 g (1 lb) dried bucatini or spaghetti

salt and freshly ground black pepper

1 tablespoon olive oil, plus more for the pasta

225 g (8 oz) guanciale or pancetta, cut into 2 cm (¾ in) cubes or strips

300 g (10½ oz) curly kale or cavolo nero (lacinato kale), leaves removed from stems, cut into 2.5 cm (1 in) ribbons (about 3 cups)

150 g (5 oz/1 cup) grated Pecorino Romano or Parmesan, plus extra for serving

Use kitchen scissors to cut the guanciale to save time.

Parmesan is a little easier to emulsify than Pecorino.

Guanciale is a bit pricier than pancetta, which might be easier to find, so either will taste great in this recipe. You could even use bacon in a pinch.

To be clear, this is not the traditional and much-loved Roman pasta, as I'm adding kale – five a day, right? Now that we've moved past that, this recipe is delicious and super easy as there are only 3 ingredients to buy, and it comes together quickly. The rendered fat from the guanciale seasons the kale and pasta, adding a pleasant saltiness to it, which goes well with the cheesy sauce.

Heat the pasta cooking water, prep the pancetta and kale during that time, then, when the pasta is cooking, grate the cheese and set the table as you'll want to eat immediately – this isn't a pasta that wants to be sitting around waiting for you to get things together.

Method

1. Fill a large pot or flameproof casserole dish (Dutch oven) with water, generously season with salt until it tastes like the sea, and bring to a vigorous boil. Add the pasta and cook, for 4 minutes less than the package instructions, about 7 minutes. The pasta should be a little too tough to bite through. Reserve 250 ml (8½ fl oz/1 cup) of pasta water, then drain into a colander in the sink and immediately drizzle with olive oil, using tongs or wooden spoon to coat the noodles so they don't stick together. Leave in the sink.

2. Wipe out the pot with a paper towel, then, over medium heat, add 1 tablespoon of the oil and the guanciale and cook, stirring occasionally, until most of the fat is rendered and pieces are brown, about 5 minutes. Add the kale, pepper and cook, stirring, until the kale wilts and starts to brown in spots, about 3–4 minutes.

3. Reduce the heat to low, then add the pasta, reserved water and cheese into the pan, stirring vigorously, until the pasta is coated with this thick, impromptu cheese sauce and is a creamy colour with little black specks that is clinging to the pasta, about 2–3 minutes more. If the pasta seems dry at any point, then add in 1 tablespoon of warm water at a time.

4. Season generously with pepper and serve immediately.

BUTTERNUT COUSCOUS
WITH CRISPY PANCETTA

Serves 4
Prep 10 minutes
Total 40 minutes

2½ tablespoons olive oil, divided

80 g (3 oz) pancetta, cut into 6 mm
(¼ in) cubes

1 medium butternut squash
(1 kg/2 lb 4 oz), peeled, seeded
and cut into 2 cm (¾ in) pieces
(page 16)

salt and freshly ground black pepper

1 shallot, thinly sliced

½ tablespoon ground cumin

1 teaspoon paprika

1 teaspoon dried red chilli flakes

2 garlic cloves, grated or minced

175 g (6 oz/1¼ cups) pearled couscous

750 ml (25 fl oz/3 cups) low-salt chicken
or vegetable stock (broth)

180 g (6½ oz/3 cups) baby spinach, or
spinach cut in half

juice of 1 lemon

15 g (½ oz/½ cup) fresh coriander
(cilantro) leaves and fine stems,
roughly chopped

30 g (1 oz/¼ cup) toasted pumpkin
seeds (page 15)

2 spring onions (scallions), white and
light green parts only, thinly sliced

Filled with tender cubes of squash, crispy bites of pancetta and crunchy pumpkin seeds, this pasta salad is a great way to sneak in some tasty vegetables. I think it tastes even better the next day (or the day after), which means you can definitely have it for lunch.

⏱ Most of the prep happens before cooking, but there will be a lot of downtime for you to clean up, hang out, toast the seeds and prep the herbs and spring onions (scallions) for serving.

Method

1. Heat ½ tablespoon of oil and the pancetta in a 30 cm (12 in) frying pan (skillet) over a medium heat and cook, stirring occasionally, until crisp and rendered, 6–7 minutes. Scrape into a bowl and set aside.

2. In the same frying pan without wiping it out, over a medium heat, add the remaining oil (there should be about 2 tablespoons in the pan, but if the pancetta has rendered a lot of fat, then reduce amount/skip added oil), add squash and season with salt, stirring frequently, until it begins to soften slightly, about 5 minutes. Add the shallot, salt and pepper, and cook, stirring frequently, until softened, about 3 minutes. Add the cumin, paprika, chilli flakes and garlic, stirring constantly until fragrant, about 1 minute. Add the couscous and stock, and raise heat to maintain an active simmer, stirring occasionally to make sure nothing is sticking to the bottom, until the couscous and squash are tender and most of the liquid is absorbed, about 12 minutes.

3. Reduce the heat to low, stir the spinach and pancetta into the pan to warm through until spinach is wilted, season to taste with salt and pepper and toss with lemon juice. Remove from heat and let sit for a few minutes to allow couscous to soak it all in, then stir in coriander. Top with the pumpkin seeds and spring onions then serve.

✏ Skip the pancetta for a veggie version, and finish it with a little Parmesan or Pecorino for a salty contrast to the slight sweetness of the butternut squash that the pancetta provided.

Butternut squash is a pain to cut. I highly recommend purchasing some pre-cut cubes if you can find them to save yourself time and effort.

GLUTEN, GRAINS AND GOOD STUFF

GARLICKY CHARRED GREENS WITH WHOLEWHEAT PENNE

Serves 4
Prep 5 minutes
Total 25 minutes

---

2 tablespoons olive oil

1 shallot, thinly sliced

salt and freshly ground black pepper

2 garlic cloves, thinly sliced or grated

½ teaspoon dried red chilli flakes

1 litre (34 fl oz/4 cups) water

500 g (1 lb) dried wholewheat or
   farro penne

600 g (1 lb 5 oz) chopped cime di rapa
   (broccoli rabe), ends trimmed and cut
   into 5 cm (2 in) pieces (about 4 cups)
   or 300 g (10½ oz) chard or cavolo nero
   (lacinato kale), leaves removed from
   stems, cut into 2.5 cm (1 in) ribbons,
   (about 3 cups)

45 g (1¾ oz/¼ cup) grated Pecorino
   Romano, plus more to serve

zest of 1 lemon

/ Garlic lovers, slice the garlic thinly so
that you get more in each bite.

I love cutting cubes of cheese and
wiggling them into the pasta as it cooks
so that they are like little surprise nuggets
when I eat it. Just putting it out there.

After reheating any leftover pasta,
squeeze in some lemon juice for
brightness, add a swirl of extra-virgin
olive oil and top with cheese.

Cime di rapa (broccoli rabe) can be a polarising vegetable as it runs on the bitter side, but I find that if you counter it with a salty fat, aka cheese, and a bit of acid, then it is actually quite enjoyable. This dish is finished under the grill (broiler) to get some char on the cime di rapa and crisp up the cheese a bit. It's kind of hard not to fight for that top layer of crunchy cime di rapa and melty cheese (the best part about testing this alone was that I got to eat the whole top layer).

 Cut the cime di rapa and clean up while the pasta is cooking.

Method

1. Heat the oil in an ovenproof 30 cm (12 in) frying pan (skillet) over a medium heat until shimmering. Add the shallot with a pinch of salt and cook until softened, about 3 minutes. Add the garlic and a pinch or more of chilli flakes, stirring constantly until fragrant but not browned, about 1 minute. Pour the water into the frying pan, raising the heat to reach a vigorous boil, then add the pasta and more salt. The water shouldn't taste like the sea as you're not draining the liquid. Cook until the pasta is al dente, about 2 minutes less than the package instructions, and stirring every few minutes to ensure nothing is sticking on the bottom, about 10 minutes. Keep tasting it as it gets closer to being done.

2. Turn on the grill to high. Place an oven rack 15 cm (6 in) from the heat source (if your grill is inside your oven).

3. Stir in the cime di rapa and then top with the grated Pecorino Romano. Here is where you'd add the little cheese nuggets, if using. Place under the grill until the cheese has melted and turned a light golden hue and the cime di rapa is starting to brown, about 2–3 minutes, depending on your grill.

4. Remove, top with lemon zest and more cheese, if desired.

FAMILY SUNDAY SUPPER: TUBULAR PASTA

Serves 4
Prep 5 minutes
Total 30 minutes

2 tablespoons olive oil, divided, plus more if needed

2 Italian-style sausages, removed from their casing

1 shallot, thinly sliced

salt and freshly ground black pepper

½–1 teaspoon dried red chilli flakes

2 x 400 g (14 oz) tins chopped tomatoes and their liquid

250 ml (8½ fl oz/1 cup) low-salt chicken stock (broth) or water

Parmesan rind (optional)

500 g (1 lb) dried fusilli, penne or small tubular-shaped pasta

185 g (6½ oz/3 cups) baby spinach

15 g (½ oz/½ cup) fresh basil, chives or mint leaves and fine stems, roughly chopped, for sprinkling

125 g (4½ oz/½ cup) ricotta, drained and lightly salted, for serving

Use any leftover ricotta for the Baked chicken and ricotta meatballs (page 38) or serve as a starter or snack: in a serving bowl, use the back of a spoon to create a shallow pool in the centre of the ricotta, drizzle in some extra-virgin olive oil, then add some freshly ground black pepper, a pinch of chilli flakes and lemon zest.

Tubular pasta is not only fun to say but it's also an ideal shape for catching the little bits of sausage. This is a great dish, along with the Less-than-an-hour ragu (page 103) for a Sunday family supper, where you can invite friends for an early dinner, sip on some wine and chat about life, forgetting the end-of-the-weekend anxiety and just enjoying each other's company.

While the pasta is cooking, cut the fresh herbs and clean up the kitchen area.

Method

1. Heat 1 tablespoon oil in a 30 cm (12 in) frying pan (skillet) over a medium-high heat until shimmering. Add the sausage, using a wooden spoon to break it up into tiny crumb-sized pieces, letting it sit and brown, then stirring every minute, until no pink is visible, and it has a nice crusty-brown exterior, about 4–6 minutes. Transfer to a bowl and set aside.

2. In the same frying pan without wiping it out, lower the heat to medium, add the remaining tablespoon of oil (if more than 2 tablespoons are left, then skip this step), then add the shallot, pinch of salt and chilli flakes. Cook until the shallot softens, about 3 minutes.

3. Add the tomatoes, stock, Parmesan rind, if using, and a pinch of salt. Raise the heat to reach an active boil, then adjust to maintain an active simmer and cook until the sauce has thickened and the strong tinned taste has cooked off, about 10 minutes. Raise the heat to a vigorous boil, add the pasta and cook, about 2 minutes less than the package directions until the pasta is al dente, roughly 7–9 minutes, stirring occasionally to make sure nothing is sticking on the bottom. Reduce the heat to low, add the sausage and spinach and cook until the sausage is warmed up and the spinach wilted, about 2 minutes more. Season to taste with salt and pepper.

4. Place in serving bowls, remove the Parmesan rind, if using, and top with ricotta, fresh herbs and some pepper.

Photo overleaf

CHEESY PASTA BAKE

Serves 4
Prep 5 minutes
Total 45 minutes

---

2 tablespoons olive oil, divided

2 Italian-style sausages, removed from their casing

3 garlic cloves, grated or minced

½–1 tablespoon dried red chilli flakes, depending on your heat preferences

2 x 400 g (14 oz) tins chopped tomatoes and their liquid

400 ml (13 fl oz/1½ cups) low-salt chicken stock (broth) or water

Parmesan rind (optional)

salt and freshly ground black pepper

500 g (1 lb) dried penne

250 g (9 oz/4 cups) baby spinach

75 g (2½ oz/½ cup) grated Parmesan

225 g (8 oz) mozzarella, torn into chunks

15 g (½ oz/½ cup) basil leaves and fine stems, sliced into thin ribbons, for sprinkling

---

/ To add more umami, add a dash of fish or soy sauce to the sauce while it's cooking; trust me on this one.

➡ For a vegetarian version, skip the sausage, add an additional 2 tablespoons olive oil to the pan and continue with garlic and chilli flakes.

During my university days, I was a bit more focused on my social life than I was on food, health and any of the things in life that I now enjoy. I would routinely order a baked ziti pasta pizza at Collegetown Pizza across the street from the bar around 1 a.m. Kelly, the manager, was my friend, mostly because I visited so often, so he would let me cut the massive line as other drunk bar-goers had the same idea, come behind the counter, hang out with the staff and get a fresh slice of this massive pizza. For some reason, I thought it was hilarious to say, 'it's two meals in one! Pasta and pizza!' As if this were a good thing. I loved pulling off the chewy, crusty pieces on top, bound together by strands of cheese and the silky bites of sauce hidden underneath. This pizza-free version is me adulting.

Method

1. Preheat the oven to 200°C (400°F/Gas 6) and put the rack in the middle.

2. Heat 1 tablespoon oil in an large ovenproof, 30 cm (12 in) frying pan (skillet) with a tight-fitting lid over a medium-high heat until shimmering. Add the sausage, using a wooden spoon to break it up into tiny crumb-sized pieces, letting it sit and brown, then stirring every minute, until no pink is visible and it has a nice crusty brown exterior, about 4–6 minutes. Transfer to a bowl and set aside.

3. In the same pan without wiping it out, add the remaining tablespoon of oil (if more than 2 tablespoons is left, then skip this step), and add the garlic and chilli flakes, stirring constantly, until fragrant but not browned, about 30 seconds. Add the tomatoes, stock, Parmesan rind, if using, a pinch of salt and adjust the heat to maintain an active simmer, until the sauce has thickened and the strong tinned taste has cooked off, about 10 minutes.

4. Raise the heat to reach a boil, then adjust the heat to maintain vigorous bubbles. Cook for 3–4 minutes less than the package instructions, stirring occasionally to make sure the pasta isn't sticking to the bottom of the pan, about 10–12 minutes – it should be a little too firm to the bite. Use this time to prep the mozzarella and spinach and do any necessary clean up.

5. Season to taste with salt and pepper, mix in the sausage, spinach, Parmesan then spread the mozzarella evenly on top. Transfer to oven and bake until cheese is melted and lightly browned, about 8–10 minutes. Top with basil and serve.

Photo on page 84

RIGATONI AND BROCCOLI
WITH CRISPY PROSCIUTTO

Serves 4
Prep 5 minutes
Total 30 minutes

---

500 g (1 lb) dried rigatoni

salt and freshly ground black pepper

2 tablespoons olive oil, plus more for the pasta

60 g (2 oz) thin slices prosciutto (about 6 slices)

2 heads broccoli and tender stems, rough ends trimmed, florets cut into bite-sized pieces, stems thinly sliced (about 350 g/12 oz/5 cups)

½ jalapeño chilli, sliced into coins

2 garlic cloves, grated or minced

½ teaspoon dried red chilli flakes

60 g (1½ oz/½ cup) grated Parmesan

juice of 1 lemon

If at any point the sauce feels dry, say when you are going back for seconds, drizzle a little more extra-virgin olive oil on top. Note: serving this type of pasta in warm bowls helps it from drying out.

Use leftover prosciutto to either snack on or make fancy scrambled eggs. Crisp them as we do here, then make the eggs in the same pan and crumble prosciutto over it. Or use in the Prosciutto-wrapped cod (page 150).

Here, we are doing a similar-ish method to the Pasta alla gricia (page 86), so if you did that one well, then you're way ahead of the game. The thing to remember is that it's important to stir well when adding the pasta, cheese and water to the pot as that's when you're creating the sauce.

While the water comes to the boil, prep the broccoli and other ingredients. Set the table and open the wine so that you can eat right away.

Method

1. Fill a large pot or casserole dish (Dutch oven) with water, generously season with salt until it tastes like the sea, and bring to a vigorous boil. Add the pasta and cook until 2 minutes shy of al dente, 4 minutes less than the package instructions. Reserve 250 ml (8½ fl oz/1 cup) of water, then drain into a colander and drizzle with oil, using tongs or wooden spoon to coat the noodles so they don't stick. Leave in the sink.

2. In the same pot, add 1 tablespoon oil over a medium heat until shimmering. Lay the prosciutto on the bottom in a single layer. Using tongs, turn once or twice until the slices tighten and crisp, about 4–5 minutes. Don't worry if they overlap a little; they will shrink a bit.

3. Remove and place the prosciutto on a paper towel-lined plate to drain. In the same pan without wiping it out, add 1 tablespoon of oil (if there's already a lot of fat/oil in there, then skip). Add the broccoli, and season with salt and pepper, stirring occasionally. Cook until it becomes crispy, about 6–8 minutes. If at any point the pot becomes too smoky, add a splash of water and use a wooden spoon to scrape up any remaining bits in the pot. Add the jalapeño, garlic, chilli flakes and a pinch of salt, stirring constantly, until fragrant, about 1 minute.

4. Reduce the heat to low, then add the pasta, reserved water and cheese to the pot, stirring vigorously until the pasta is coated with a thick, impromptu cheese sauce and is a creamy colour that is clinging to the pasta, about 2–3 minutes more. Crumble in half of the prosciutto. If the pasta seems dry at any point, then add 1 tablespoon warm water at a time. Off heat, stir in the lemon juice. Crumble the rest of the prosciutto on top with some pepper and serve.

Photo overleaf

BAKED EGGS AND BARLEY

WITH PEPPERS, GREENS AND GOAT'S CHEESE

Serves 2, 4 for sharing
Prep 10 minutes
Total 40 minutes

2 tablespoons olive oil

1 medium red onion, diced

2 orange and red (bell) peppers, seeded and diced

300 g (10½ oz/2 cups) baby plum (grape) tomatoes, halved

salt and freshly ground black pepper

½ teaspoon dried red chilli flakes

200 g (7 oz/1 cup) barley

900 ml (30½ fl oz/3½ cups) low-salt vegetable stock (broth) or water

150 g (5 oz) leafy greens such as kale or chard, leaves removed from stems, cut into 2.5 cm (1 in) ribbons (about 2 packed cups)

zest and juice of 2 lemons

4 eggs

75 g (2½ oz/½ cup) goat's cheese, crumbled

15 g (½ oz/½ cup) parsley leaves and fine stems, roughly chopped, for sprinkling

I prefer orange, yellow or red peppers to green, but you can mix and match to your preferred tastes. You can also use chard stem ends for this recipe – just trim the very base.

A colourful hodgepodge of ingredients that you will want to dig into anytime of the day or week. Baked eggs are easy, gorgeous, and you can bring the pan to the table or eat it solo out of the pan if that's your style (been there, done that).

Use the barley cooking time to prep the greens and zest the lemon. Chop the herbs while the eggs are cooking and set the table.

Method

1. Heat the oil in an ovenproof 30 cm (12 in) frying pan (skillet) with a tight-fitting lid over a medium heat until shimmering. Add the onion, peppers, tomatoes, and season with salt and pepper. Cook, stirring frequently, until everything has softened and the tomatoes have started to blister, about 5 minutes. Add chilli flakes, stirring constantly until fragrant, about 30 seconds.

2. Add the barley and toast for about 1 minute – this makes it tastier – then add the stock and a pinch more salt and cover. Raise the heat to bring to a vigorous boil, then the remove lid and adjust the heat to maintain an active simmer and cook uncovered until most of the water has been absorbed and the barley is just tender, about 15 minutes, stirring every few minutes to make sure nothing is sticking to the bottom.

3. Turn on the grill (broiler) with the rack 15 cm (6 in) from the heat source (if your grill is inside your oven).

4. Stir the greens into the barley until they start to wilt, then add juice from 1 lemon. Using a wooden spoon, create four wells in the barley and crack the eggs inside them. Crumble the cheese all over and place under the grill until the eggs whites are set and the yolks are runny, about 5–6 minutes, depending on your grill. Once the time gets close, check on the eggs every 30 seconds by jiggling the pan to see if the whites are firm or still loose.

5. Top with lemon zest, pepper and parsley and squeeze the remaining lemon juice all over.

Photo overleaf

LESS-THAN-AN-HOUR RAGU

Serves 4
Prep 10 minutes
Total 50 minutes

---

3 tablespoons olive oil, divided

125 g (4 oz/¼ lb) pancetta, finely chopped

350 g (12 oz/¾ lb) lean beef mince (ground beef)

salt and freshly ground black pepper

1 carrot, peeled and diced

1 celery stalk, diced

1 small red onion, chopped

2 garlic cloves, grated or minced

½ teaspoon dried chilli flakes or more, depending on heat preference

120 ml (4 fl oz/½ cup) red wine

2 x 400 g (14 oz) tins whole peeled tomatoes and their liquid

250 ml (8½ fl oz/1 cup) water

Parmesan rind (optional)

450 g (1 lb) dried spaghetti

grated Parmesan, for sprinkling

15 g (½ oz/½ cup) basil leaves and fine stems, roughly torn or sliced, to serve (optional)

✐ While the onion/carrot/celery don't need to be perfectly cut like a fine-dining restaurant (I always judge myself on that), try to make them small and similar in size so that they cook evenly.

'Eat with your hands, it's good for you', my aunt said something along those lines to me when, as a kid, a variation of this dish was set in front of me without any cutlery. It was one of the more fun and freeing moments of my childhood and something I still try to emulate today, as she was right, it does feel good to break conventional rules every now and then.

Another great Sunday supper dish, this is my untraditional version of bolognese that can be done in under an hour but still has that warming, cosy feeling that a nice bowl of tomato-and-meat slicked pasta provides.

⏱ First chop the pancetta, then, while the pancetta/beef cooks, prep the carrots, celery and onion, making sure to check back on the meat as you're chopping.

Method

1. Heat 1 tablespoon of the olive oil in a flameproof casserole dish (Dutch oven) over a medium-high heat until shimmering. Add the pancetta, beef and a little salt (the pancetta will add some salt) and pepper, breaking the meat up into tiny, crumb-sized pieces with a wooden spoon throughout the cooking process. Let the meat get contact with the pan before stirring so that it browns, then stir occasionally and cook until there is no pink remaining, the meat is browned all over, and the pancetta is crispy with most of the fat rendered, about 10–12 minutes. Place in a mixing bowl and set aside.

2. In the same pot without wiping it out, reduce to medium heat and add the remaining olive oil (reduce the amount or skip if there is already a layer of liquid across the surface of the pan) until shimmering. Add the carrot, celery, onion and salt cooking until softened, about 6–8 minutes. Add the garlic and chilli flakes, cooking until fragrant, about 30 seconds. Pour in the red wine, scraping up any brown bits left on the bottom of the pan, letting it cook until the pan looks almost dry again with very little liquid left, about 3 minutes.

Continued on the next page

3. Add the tomatoes and water, letting them soften for about 2 minutes, then gently smashing and breaking up the tomatoes with the back of a wooden spoon or potato masher. Season with salt and pepper. Add the Parmesan rind, if using. Raise the heat to bring the liquid to an active boil, then adjust to maintain an active simmer, letting the tinned taste cook off and sauce thicken, about 10 minutes. Season to taste.

4. Add the pasta and adjust the heat level to maintain an active boil and cook until the pasta is just barely al dente and is a touch too firm, 3 minutes before the package says – so roughly 7–9 minutes. Stir occasionally to make sure nothing is sticking on the bottom.

5. Stir the meat and any liquid into the bowl back to the pan, until the meat warms up and pasta is al dente, about 2 minutes more. Season to taste.

6. Divide between plates and top with Parmesan and basil.

FANCY WEEKNIGHT MUSHROOM PASTA

Serves 2, 4 for sharing
Prep 5 minutes
Total 20 minutes

---

salt and freshly ground black pepper

450 g (1 lb) dried wholewheat penne

2 tablespoons olive oil, plus more for the pasta

450 g (1 lb) mixed mushrooms, woody stems removed and cut into thin slices (about 2¼ cups)

2 garlic cloves, thinly sliced

100 g (3½ oz/¾ cup) grated Parmesan, plus extra to serve

juice of 1 lemon

15 g (½ oz/½ cup) fresh parsley or basil leaves and fine stems, hand torn or roughly chopped

---

i This is the same mushroom-cooking method from page 56. Read that recipe for more mushroom prep tips before you make this.

If you find reserving the pasta water tricky, then use tongs to transfer the pasta into the colander, drizzle it with oil and then reserve some water before draining. You can also save the water to boil vegetables as a side dish.

Add water to the pan when reheating and stir in quick-cooking greens once hot, so you feel like you're eating a different dish.

This is a weeknight staple for me because it is so simple to make yet looks kind of fancy with the mixture of mushrooms and bright green of the herbs.

Boil the water (you can use a kettle to speed up the process. I heat up a tiny bit of water on high as the kettle boils so the pan is already hot), then prep the mushrooms and garlic while the water boils and the pasta cooks.

Method

1. Fill a large flameproof casserole dish (Dutch oven) or wide, heavy frying pan (skillet) with water and bring to a vigorous boil, salting it until it tastes like the sea. Add the pasta, making sure it is submerged, and cook for 3–4 minutes less than the package instructions so that it's just shy of al dente, about 6 minutes. Reserve 250 ml (8½ fl oz/1 cup) water, then drain the pasta into a colander in the sink. Immediately drizzle with olive oil, using tongs or wooden spoons to toss it. This stops the pasta from sticking together.

2. Wipe out the pot with a paper towel. Heat it over a medium-high heat until very hot. To test, add a drop of water, and it will sizzle when hot. Add the mushrooms to the dry pan and let them cook, untouched for 1 minute, as they release water, shrink and brown, then stir. I know it can feel torturous and tempting not to move them around as you'll hear them sizzle, but try to wait at least 1 minute between each stir, until they've all shrunken in size and are a golden brown, about 5–6 minutes.

3. Pour in 2 tablespoons of olive oil, garlic and salt, stirring constantly, until the garlic becomes more transparent than white, about 2 minutes. Pour in the pasta, half the reserved pasta water and the cheese, stirring vigorously until a thick, creamy sauce forms, about 2 minutes. If it's not as creamy as you'd like, then add a tablespoon more of the pasta water at a time.

4. Finish with the lemon juice, parsley and pepper, then season to taste with salt. Divide between plates and top with a drizzle of oil, if desired. Serve with more cheese.

I HAVE A THING FOR FETA

A quick search of my recipes online reveals a pretty common theme (hint: it's feta). Blame it on my dad. Growing up, he would have what we called *noon eh paneer*, which translates to bread and cheese, every Saturday and Sunday for lunch. It was something from his childhood, and his Americanised version was to get a fresh sourdough baguette from a shop near our house, wash fresh herbs, such as basil and mint, either from his garden in the summer or from the shop in winter, sliced cherry tomatoes (Sungolds in the summer, if we were lucky) and a huge block of Bulgarian feta. He'd slice and warm the bread for us, place it in a bread basket and cover it with a cloth to keep it warm. Then, we'd watch and follow suit as he took out a small piece, opened it up and made a little sandwich by spreading the cheese inside, adding a few sprigs of herbs, sliced tomatoes and then eat and repeat. He still does it to this day, and, as simple as it sounds, it's delicious. There's something so gratifying about making little sandwiches yourself, as if it's a little game that you get to play over and over again.

Now, why do I prefer Bulgarian feta? Well, obviously because it's the best. Let me explain why. Here is a quick breakdown of the feta types that you are probably most familiar with.

Greek feta: Comes from Greece, made in a traditional Greek method with all or mostly all sheep's milk and 30 per cent or less goat's milk. It has a Protected Designation of Origin, much like Champagne, which is why technically it's the only one that is supposed to be called feta.

French feta: It's made with sheep's milk leftover from the production of Roquefort, causing it to have a sharper flavour profile.

Bulgarian feta: It can be made with sheep, cow or goat's milk (or sometimes different combinations of them) and is tart, tangy and creamy.

I find that Bulgarian feta in the brine (the murky, cloudy and salty liquid you see it bathing in) is the the tastiest of all of them. You, of course, are entitled to your own opinion, but keep in mind that these recipes were all developed using Bulgarian for that extra creaminess and tang that is not present in French or Greek fetas. That said, it can be a little tricky to source Bulgarian feta in the UK, but if you can get your hands on a block it is well worth it. Feta in a brine is the second best alternative.

If anyone knows how I can become a sponsor for Bulgarian feta, then please do tell. I'm available.

LEMONY ORZO

WITH PRAWNS, ASPARAGUS AND FETA

Serves 2, 4 for sharing
Prep 5 minutes
Total 25 minutes

---

salt and freshly ground black pepper

200 g (7 oz/1 cup) orzo

2 tablespoons olive oil, plus more for the pasta

2 garlic cloves, grated or minced

½ teaspoon dried red chilli flakes

250 g (9 oz) asparagus, ends trimmed and cut into 2.5 cm (1 in) pieces (about 2 cups)

10–12 peeled medium prawns (shrimp), deveined (about 450 g/1 lb)

2 teaspoons dried oregano

15 g (½ oz/½ cup) fresh basil or parsley leaves and fine stems, roughly chopped

juice of 2 lemons

1 tablespoon extra-virgin olive oil

75 g (2½ oz/½ cup) feta (preferably Bulgarian), crumbled

Prawns can quickly go from tender and delicious to rubbery and unpleasant if overcooked. Keep a close watch on timing and how they look, perhaps even cut off a small piece to try if you're unsure, to avoid this sad fate.

Swap the asparagus for broccoli florets, peas or other crunchy, quick-cooking green vegetables you can sauté in the frying pan (skillet).

Whenever I'm in Greece, my goal is to have a Greek salad or really anything that involves feta as often as possible – you could also argue that I do this when not in Greece. This Greek-inspired dish is my at-home version that gets a bit of a textural crunch and boost of colour from asparagus, for a bright, lemony pasta dish. You could also add in some sliced baby plum (grape) tomatoes with the asparagus to make it saucier.

Prep the ingredients while you bring the water to a boil and while the orzo is cooking. Use this time to toss the prawns with the oregano.

Method

1. Fill a 30 cm (12 in) frying pan (skillet) or flameproof casserole dish (Dutch oven) two-thirds of the way with water, salt to taste like the sea and bring to a vigorous boil over a high heat. Add the orzo and cook according to package instructions until just shy of al dente, about 7–9 minutes, stirring occasionally. Drain into a colander in the sink, then run through with olive oil, using a wooden spoon to stir, and leave in the sink or transfer to a bowl.

2. Wipe out the frying pan with a paper towel and return to a medium-high heat. Add 2 tablespoons of the oil and heat until shimmering. Add the garlic and chilli flakes and cook, stirring constantly, until fragrant but not browned, about 30 seconds. Add the asparagus, season with salt and pepper and stir to coat. Cook until the asparagus is tender but retains a crisp bite, about 3–4 minutes, stirring occasionally. Meanwhile, toss the prawns with the oregano to coat. Move the asparagus to the sides of the frying pan and add the prawns. Cook, turning the prawns occasionally, until they are pink and no longer translucent, about 3–4 minutes.

3. Reduce the heat to medium, return the orzo back to the frying pan, along with most of the basil, the lemon juice, extra-virgin olive oil and most of the feta, stirring to combine, until the orzo is warmed up, about 1–2 minutes more. Adjust seasoning with salt and pepper as needed, then top with remaining basil and feta and serve immediately.

Photo overleaf

TOMATO RICE

WITH CHICKEN AND GREEN BEANS

Serves 4
Prep 5 minutes
Total 45 minutes

---

2 tablespoons olive oil

1 large yellow onion, diced

salt and freshly ground black pepper

1 teaspoon ground turmeric

450 g (1 lb) skinless, boneless
　chicken thighs

500 g (1 lb 2 oz/2 cups) passata
　(strained tomatoes)

500 ml (17 fl oz/2 cups) water

200 g (7 oz/1 cup) basmati rice or other
　long-grain rice, rinsed

150 g (5¼ oz/1 cup) frozen cut green
　beans, sliced into 5 cm (2 in) pieces

Greek yoghurt or labneh, for serving

---

*To save time, use shredded leftover or rotisserie chicken and add to the tomato rice at the same point the pulled chicken is added in the recipe.

Make sure to use the correct amount of passata as too little will undercook the rice.

As a kid, I went through a phase of hating green beans. This was particularly troubling when my parents made a Persian dish called *loobia polow* that consists of green beans, chunks of beef, tomato and rice – it's delicious. But, very problematic at the time, as the cut-up green beans are all up in there. Now, as a *mature* adult, I love this dish for its simplicity and warming taste. This recipe is more of a hybrid of that one and a tomato rice that my dad makes. It's comforting and hearty without being heavy, and is perfect for cold nights.

⏱ Use the chicken poaching and rice cooking downtime to do the little things you need to do like putting laundry away, cleaning the kitchen or calling your friend to catch up. Just make sure to set a timer on your phone.

Method

1. Heat the oil in a flameproof casserole dish (Dutch oven) or large frying pan (skillet) with a tight-fitting lid over a medium heat until shimmering. Add the onion and a pinch of salt and cook, stirring frequently, until softened, about 4 minutes. Stir in the turmeric, cooking until fragrant, about 1 minute. Season the chicken generously with salt and pepper. Add to the pan along with the passata and water, adjust heat to maintain an active simmer (avoid bringing it to a boil). Simmer until the chicken is cooked through, about 10 minutes, stirring occasionally, turning it over if not completely submerged. Use tongs to remove the chicken, holding it over the pot to drain any liquid, then place in a shallow bowl or plate.

2. Add the rice and salt then raise the heat to maintain an active simmer. Cover and cook until the rice is soft and most of the liquid has been absorbed, about 15–20 minutes, stirring to make sure nothing sticks to the bottom. Keep the heat low to avoid burning and try to open the lid as little as possible. Add more water, if necessary, in 125 ml (½ cup) increments. Use this time to shred the chicken with a fork and knife. When the rice is ready, stir in the green beans, chicken, and any liquid, until the beans are soft and the chicken warm, about 3 minutes. Cover and let sit for 5 minutes off the heat. Adjust seasoning as needed then serve with the yoghurt.

PEARLED COUSCOUS

WITH MUSSELS

Serves 2, 4 for sharing
Prep 15 minutes
Total 45 minutes

---

2 tablespoons olive oil

1 shallot, thinly sliced

salt and freshly ground black pepper

½ teaspoon dried red chilli flakes

2 x 400 g (14 oz) tins chopped tomatoes
and their liquid

250 ml (8½ fl oz/1 cup) water

175 g (6 oz/1¼ cups) pearled couscous

450 g (1 lb) mussels, debearded and
scrubbed (page 60)

15 g (½ oz/½ cup) basil or parsley leaves
and fine stems, roughly chopped,
for sprinkling

15 g (½ oz/½ cup) chives, finely
chopped, for sprinkling (optional)

Swap the couscous for a more traditional pasta; just adjust the cooking time and heat level so that there are active bubbles versus a simmer, and add mussels 5 minutes before noodles are done.

My favourite way to eat mussels is a method I learned from a French girl who I once saw doing this in a café: it's using an empty mussel shell to pluck out the mussel from another, Pac-Man style, kind of like a piner-claw-thing that extends from my hand. It feels like I'm playing a game while I eat and is a lot easier (and more fun) than using a fork. She then neatly stacked her discarded shells, tucking one in to another like shopping carts. That felt a little too organised for me, but do what suits you.

Debeard the mussels while the tomatoes and pasta cook. If they are beard-less, then use this free time to do something fun you might not otherwise have done. Or play on your phone.

Method

1. Heat the oil in a flameproof casserole dish (Dutch oven) over a medium-high heat until shimmering. Add the shallot and a pinch of salt and cook until softened, about 2 minutes. Add the chilli flakes, tomatoes and water. Raise the heat to achieve an active boil, then adjust to maintain an active simmer. Season with salt and pepper. Cook until the tomatoes naturally break apart and the sauce thickens slightly, about 10 minutes.

2. Stir in the couscous, then adjust the heat to maintain an active simmer and cook until the couscous is just tender and most of the sauce has been absorbed, about 12 minutes. Use this time to clean up the kitchen or have a glass of wine. Season the sauce to taste with salt and pepper, keeping in mind that the mussels will add a bit of salt of their own.

3. Stir in the mussels, cover and cook until most of the mussels have opened, using a wooden spoon to stir once to make sure nothing is sticking on the bottom, about 5 minutes. Use this time to prep the herbs.

4. Discard any unopen mussels. Divide between serving plates, setting out a bowl for the empty shells, and garnish with herbs.

MY MAMA'S CHICKEN

Serves 4
Prep 10 minutes
Total 35 minutes

---

4 skin-on, bone-in chicken thighs
   (about 675 g/1½ lb)

1 teaspoon ground cumin

3 tablespoons olive oil, divided

¼ teaspoon saffron threads

1 tablespoon hot water

salt and freshly ground black pepper

500 ml (17 fl oz/2 cups) low-salt chicken
   stock (broth) or water

200 g (7 oz/1 cup) basmati rice, rinsed

2 lemons, juice of 1, 1 cut into wedges,
   for serving

15 g (½ oz/½ cup) fresh parsley or
   coriander (cilantro) leaves and fine
   stems, roughly chopped, for sprinkling

Growing up in my house we had a running joke, 'what's for dinner?... chicken!' My mother is not someone who enjoys cooking, even though she's very good at it. It's ironic because both my sister and I have pursued careers in food. My dad is the one who loves cooking and instilled that appreciation in us. Regardless, it was very important to both our parents that we ate well and always had dinner together as a family.

Inevitably, what was at the centre of this dinner was some form of chicken dish. My mother made a chicken stir fry, a roasted 'chicken with greens' (Cornish hens coated in dried oregano and other herbs) and 'lemon chicken' (roasted Cornish hens in a lemon and saffron bath with whole black peppercorns and red potatoes). All were served with fluffy basmati rice.

This recipe is inspired by these dishes, as it's a one-pot combination of seared chicken that's finished on top of a bed of lemon-saffron rice. The idea is to get a nice colour on the chicken and add some of their rendered tasty bits to the overall dish as they will finish cooking with the rice. As a note, the skin will get a little soft during the cook process, but will still taste delicious. Though the rice ends up being softer than traditional Persian rice, the taste and smell are undeniably as rich and wonderful as my childhood memories.

Method

1. Season the chicken all over with salt, pepper and cumin. Heat 2 tablespoons of the oil in a large frying pan (skillet) with a tight-fitting lid over a medium-high heat until very hot – less of a gentle, wavy shimmer and more like aggressive lava when you move the pan. Add the chicken, skin-side down, and cook without moving until it easily releases from the pan, and skin is crispy and well browned, about 4–7 minutes. (Test the chicken at 4 minutes to check its resistance.) Use tongs to flip and brown the other side, about 3–6 minutes longer. Transfer chicken to a plate and set aside.

2. Meanwhile, in the bottom of a small metal or sturdy bowl, grind the saffron and mix with hot water until dissolved.

Continued on the next page

Pull the chicken off the bone for sandwiches or to serve on top of salad.

For an easy soup, heat low-salt stock with chopped vegetables such as potatoes or carrots, and, when cooked, add leafy greens and shredded chicken to warm up for 5 minutes.

If you find yourself chicken-less, heat up the rice, crack an egg in it and make a quick-fried rice, stirring in baby spinach and serve with sambal.

3. Reduce the heat to medium and add the chicken stock to the same pan, scraping up anything stuck to the bottom with a wooden spoon. Add the rice, juice of 1 lemon and saffron water then season with salt and stir to combine. There will probably be a little fat in the pan, which is great. If it's charred or black though, rinse it out quickly and add 1 tablespoon of the oil to the rice/stock mixture.

4. Cover with the lid, bring the liquid to an active boil and then lower the heat to maintain an active simmer. Remove the lid and lay the chicken, skin-side up, carefully on top. Cover and cook until the rice is tender, most of the liquid is absorbed and the chicken has finished cooking, about 15–20 minutes. Use this time to clean up, set the table and make sure your pepper mill is stocked.

5. Remove the rice from the heat, fluff with a fork, cover and let it sit for a few minutes while you prep the herbs. Divide between plates and finish with loads of pepper. Top with the herbs and serve with lemon wedges.

COCONUT RICE
WITH PRAWNS AND COURGETTES

Serves 2, 4 for sharing
Prep 10 minutes
Total 40 minutes

---

2 tablespoons olive oil

2 courgettes (zucchini), cut into 1 cm
(½ in) pieces (about 2 cups)

salt and freshly ground black pepper

10–12 peeled prawns (shrimp), deveined
(about 450 g/1 lb)

1 jalapeño chilli, sliced into coins

2 spring onions (scallions), light green
and white parts only, thinly sliced

3 teaspoons low-salt soy sauce

200 g (7 oz/1 cup) basmati or other
long-grain rice, rinsed

400 ml (13.5 fl oz) tin light
coconut milk

250 ml (8½ fl oz/1 cup) water

1 teaspoon fish sauce

3 limes, 2 for juice, 1 sliced in wedges,
to serve

15 g (½ oz/½ cup) fresh coriander
(cilantro) leaves and fine stems,
roughly chopped, for sprinkling

Make this vegetarian by skipping
the prawns and stirring in mangetout
(snow peas) when the courgettes are
added back into the pan.

Add oil to a hot pan, mix in the rice
until warm and stir in 1–2 eggs to make
a delicious, crispy fried rice dish.

This dish is sort of like a risotto in that the rice is soft
and kind of like *risi e bisi*, the Venetian spring dish that's
made with peas mixed in, except we use courgettes in this
recipe. So basically, it's not like either of those. It is a dish
that instantly makes you feel warm and cosy. It's probably
because the rice is cooked in light coconut milk, which lends
a richness to it, and fresh herbs for a bright dinner that
comes together quickly.

Most of the prep needs to happen fast, so you'll have downtime
when the rice is cooking. You can use that time to set the table, cut
the limes, drink some wine or play on your phone. Your call.

Method

1. Heat the oil over a medium-high heat in a flameproof casserole
dish (Dutch oven) with a tight-fitting lid until shimmering. Add the
courgettes and season with salt, stirring occasionally, until they start
to char and brown on the outside, about 5 minutes. Use a wooden
spoon to push to the sides of the pan, then add the prawns, letting
them have direct contact with the pan for 1 minute. Then add half
of the chilli and the whites of the spring onions, stirring everything
together. Cook until the prawns are barely pink all over, about
2 minutes. You want them slightly undercooked. Add 1 teaspoon soy
sauce to the pan, mix it around with the wooden spoon so it coats
the ingredients, then transfer to a small bowl and set aside.

2. In the same pot without wiping it out, add the rice, coconut
milk, water and season again with salt, using a wooden spoon to stir
together. Cover and raise the heat to bring it to an active boil, then
adjust the heat to maintain an active simmer, cooking until the rice is
soft and most of the liquid has been absorbed, about 15–20 minutes.
Be sure to keep the heat low so that the rice doesn't burn. Stir once
in a while to make sure nothing is sticking to the bottom.

3. Stir in the courgette and prawn mixture, remaining soy sauce
and fish sauce. Cook uncovered until warmed up, about 2 minutes.
Off the heat, stir in the lime juice and adjust the seasoning to taste.
Divide in bowls and top with coriander, the greens of the spring
onions and remaining chilli, if desired. Serve with lime wedges.

DILL RICE
WITH BROAD BEANS AND SMOKED FISH

Serves 2, 4 for sharing
Prep 10 minutes
Total 30 minutes

---

200 g (7 oz/1 cup) basmati rice or other long-grained rice, rinsed

500 ml (17 fl oz/2 cups) water

1 tablespoon olive oil or ghee

salt

225 g (8 oz) smoked fish, such as mackerel or salmon, flaked

150 g (5 oz/1 cup) frozen or fresh shelled broad (lima) or edamame beans

1 large bunch dill, leaves and stems roughly chopped (about 1 cup)

Greek yoghurt, for serving

1 lemon, cut into wedges, for serving

Top with a fried egg or two 6-minute eggs – ones that have been in boiling water for exactly that length of time, then put in an ice bath or run under cold water to stop the cooking process. The whites will be set but the yolks will be runny, so they'll act as an impromptu sauce and akin to Kedgeree, the British breakfast dish with curried rice, smoked fish and eggs (one of my favourites).

Use any leftover dill in the Warm couscous salad with salmon and mustard-dill dressing (page 124).

This is a hybrid of a Persian dish that's served with smoked fish on the side rather than mixed in (and usually has a crispy bottom). I love the fresh taste of the chopped dill, which makes the whole dish feel alive (if that word can be used to describe cooked food). It's great to eat in both warm and cold weather as it straddles the line of something filling yet light.

I find flaking the fish with my hands to be quicker and more fun; plus, I can more easily spot any stray pin bones, but it will leave a little stink on your hands – squeeze fresh lemon juice directly on them to remove the smell and then wash your hands as normal. I also do this after eating lobster or other shellfish Pac-Man style (page 111).

Chop the dill (it will smell so good) and flake the fish while the rice is cooking to pretty much eliminate all prep time.

Method

1. In a flameproof casserole dish (Dutch oven) or large frying pan (skillet) with a tight-fitting lid, combine the rice, water and oil, then season well with the salt. (You're not draining the water so you don't want it to taste like the sea.) Cover and bring the water to an active boil, then reduce the heat to maintain an active simmer, keep covered and cook until most of the liquid has been absorbed, about 15–20 minutes. Try not to peek under too much until the end and keep the heat low so it doesn't burn.

2. Stir in the broad beans and dill until you see green-speckled rice rather than solo white grains. Cook until the beans are warmed through, about 5 minutes more. Remove from the heat, fluff the rice with a fork and then stir in the smoked fish and cover while you set the table, about 5 minutes. Serve with lots of yoghurt and lemon wedges.

SALAD
FOR
DINNER

SPRINKLES
ON THE SIDE

One of my goals as a child was to be a 'regular' somewhere. And, I eventually decided that Friendly's, an American diner-ish chain known for ice cream, was going to be it. There was one not too far from our house growing up, so, during the summer, my parents would take us to get ice cream. Every time, I ordered black raspberry in a sugar cone with chocolate sprinkles on top and in a cup on the side (so I could dip it in after I licked off the top layer, and so on, obviously) until someone, anyone, would say, 'the usual?' I was relentless in my ordering.

And then it happened.

One might even say it was a life-defining moment. Hello, achieving goals, left and right. We were sitting in a booth and the young female server looked at me and said, 'the usual for you?' I nodded, trying to play it cool, though I'm sure my face lit up, probably looking like the greatest thing on earth had just happened to me. I don't know if my parents or sister had any idea of this secret dream, or why I was so excited. I probably didn't share either.

Sadly, my glory days were short lived as we found out not too long after that I had genetic high cholesterol (familial hypercholesterolemia), so I had to switch to frozen yoghurt – a chocolate and vanilla swirl on a wafer cone with sprinkles on it and on the side.

While it does suck in certain ways (most notably in crushing my childhood dream), I'm really grateful as it made me be more aware of the need for balance in my life and diet at an early age. I became more mindful of how I felt both physically and emotionally, and what I was feeding myself to help manage both of those things. It's probably because I knew that I needed to always eat a lot of vegetables, lean meats, fruits, seafood and avoid cholesterol-rich foods like cream, butter and fatty meats that I began to prefer and love them – though we can safely say that my university years were a giant blip in this entire thing.

Vegetarian and lean dishes are scattered throughout the book, but this particular section is in celebration of the salad and all the different ways that it can be enjoyed, like the Charred lettuce with prawns and feta dressing (page 129) with crisp browned leaves tossed in a cheesy dressing and the Panzanella salad with rocket and crispy Parmesan (page 122) topped with addictive salty rounds of fricos. Seriously, once you make them you won't stop. I *had* to test them four times to make sure they were just right.

You'll notice that the proteins in these recipes can be swapped around (or left out) as there are basic instructions for most of them. For example, you can serve prawns (shrimp) on top of the Caesar or steak with the charred corn, tomato and avocado salad, just prepare the proteins as directed and mix and match to your liking.

I hope that these Salad for Dinner recipes help when you feel like you need a little more balance in life. Or, when you just want to eat a salad for dinner.

GOOD TO KNOW

For Salads: To keep the dirty dishes to a minimum, make the dressing in the bottom of the serving bowl so that you can toss the ingredients directly in there, rather than using a mixing bowl. If it looks too messy for your liking, take a paper towel and wipe around the inside of the bowl for a *fresh* appearance.

Make Ahead: Make the dressing the night before, store in a jam jar or something similar, then shake and use. It will last a day or two in the fridge.

PANZANELLA SALAD
WITH ROCKET AND CRISPY PARMESAN

Serves 2, 4 for sharing
Prep 10 minutes
Total 25 minutes

1 garlic clove, grated or minced

1 teaspoon Dijon mustard

2 tablespoons red wine vinegar

3 tablespoons extra-virgin olive oil

salt and freshly ground black pepper

450 g (1 lb/3 cups) stale bread cubes, preferably toasted (page 81)

900 g (2 lb/4 cups) tomatoes, halved or quartered

1 small red onion, thinly sliced

15 g (½ oz/½ cup) fresh basil leaves, sliced or roughly torn

80 g (3 oz/¾ cup) grated Parmesan or more, if desired

120 g (4 oz/2 cups) baby rocket (arugula)

---

*Use bread with a crunchy crust for this dish so you have that textural element in the salad rather than soggy pieces of bread. The better quality the bread, the better the salad, of course.

➜ Play around with any ingredients you have on hand, adding in sliced cucumbers, peppers or chickpeas (garbanzo beans).

Leftover fricos make a great cocktail snack.

When I was a food editor, I ran a cooking challenge with the staff. Each week, I picked a different ingredient and everyone had to develop a recipe using it. Often times, myself, Maryse and Molly, the drink and restaurant editors, respectively, did ours together, enjoying wine and helping each other develop (and eat) them. During one session, as we were eating, Molly started talking about fricos in passing and, as she continued talking, Maryse and I looked at each other and interrupted with a, 'what now?' Molly looked at us like we were the crazy ones, not believing that we didn't know what fricos were. She explained that they were grated Parmesan piles that you bake in the oven to get crispy. A quick internet search revealed that she was right, and she immediately responded with, 'you've been foodied, b*tch!' She was watching a lot of *Breaking Bad* at the time and doesn't usually speak this way, which is one reason why it was so hilarious that she said that. Ever since, I feel like I spot them all the time and can't help but giggle when I think of both her and that night. Let's please make this phrase a thing.

Method

1. Preheat the oven to 190°C (375°F/Gas 5) with the rack in the middle.

2. In the bottom of a serving bowl, combine the garlic, mustard, red wine vinegar and extra-virgin olive oil then season with salt and pepper. Toss in the bread, tomatoes, onion and basil, making sure all are coated well with the dressing. Set aside at room temperature. Do not refrigerate.

3. Line a baking tray (sheet pan) with baking parchment. Spoon 1 tablespoon of the cheese onto the parchment, forming a small mound, then use the back of the spoon to flatten them if they are really high, otherwise they will be sticky, not crunchy. Continue 1 tablespoon at a time, placing each mound at least 5 cm (2 in) from the other (they will spread out as they bake). Top each with pepper. Place in the oven and bake until a golden brown, about 9–10 minutes. You don't want them to become too dark or they will taste bitter. Immediately use a metal spatula to gently pry them off the paper. Allow to cool for 2 minutes. Add the rocket to the salad, then top with the fricos and serve.

WARM COUSCOUS SALAD
WITH SALMON AND MUSTARD-DILL DRESSING

Serves 2, 4 for sharing
Prep 5 minutes
Total 30 minutes

---

2 x 225 g (8 oz) skin-on salmon fillets

salt and freshly ground black pepper

4 tablespoons olive oil, divided

1 medium shallot, thinly sliced

175 g (6 oz/1¼ cups) pearled couscous

750 ml (25 fl oz/3 cups) low-salt chicken
  or vegetable stock (broth)

150 g (5 oz/1 cup) frozen shelled broad
  (lima) beans or edamame beans

2 tablespoons Dijon mustard

juice of 1 lemon

15 g (½ oz/½ cup) picked fresh dill
  leaves and fine stems, roughly
  chopped, plus more for sprinkling

60 g (2 oz/1 cup) baby spinach

2 spring onions (scallions), white and
  light green parts only, thinly sliced,
  for sprinkling

Use any leftover dill in the Dill
rice with broad beans and smoked fish
(page 116).

I love chopping dill; I not only find the task relaxing, but
I also find it immensely satisfying to hear the crunch of
the leaves beneath my knife and to watch the pile shrink
down from a wild mess to something clean and pretty.
And the fragrance emitted by the herbs reminds me of my
childhood, when I'd walk into the house and see my mother
and grandmother laboriously chopping mountains of dills to
make my favourite dish, *ghormeh-sabzi*, which is stewed beef
with loads of fresh herbs.

Cook the salmon, then the couscous, using the downtime to prep
the beans. Make the dressing and then cut the dill and spring onions
(scallions), and flake the salmon. Use the remaining time to clean up.

Method

1. Season salmon with salt and pepper. Heat half the oil in a
30 cm (12 in) frying pan (skillet) over a medium-high heat until
shimmering. Add the salmon, skin-side down, and immediately
reduce the heat to medium-low. Cook, gently pressing down all over
gently with a spatula to ensure contact, until the skin is rendered and
crisp, about 6 minutes. If you feel resistance when attempting to lift
with a spatula, allow it to continue to cook until it lifts easily.

2. Flip the salmon and cook until an instant-read thermometer
inserted into the thickest part registers 50°C (120°F) for medium
rare or 55°C (130°F) for medium, about 1–2 minutes longer. Transfer
the salmon to a paper towel-lined plate and allow to cool. Once
cooled, flake the salmon using your hands or a fork; discard the skin
or crumble it into the dish. If your hands smell then squeeze some
lemon juice over them before rinsing with water.

3. Meanwhile, wipe out the pan with a paper towel. Add the
remaining 2 tablespoons of oil and heat over medium heat until
shimmering. Add the shallot and a pinch of salt then cook until
softened, about 2 minutes. Add the couscous and cook, stirring, until
lightly toasted and fragrant, about 1 minute. Add the stock, stirring to
combine and scraping up any brown bits on the bottom of the pan,
and raise heat then adjust it to maintain an active simmer. Cook until
most of the liquid has been absorbed and the couscous is tender,
about 12 minutes. During the last 6 minutes of cooking, stir in the
beans and a pinch of salt. Strain any excess liquid.

4. Meanwhile, in a large serving bowl, mix together the mustard and lemon juice. Stir in the couscous, along with dill and spinach, stirring to fluff the couscous and wilt the spinach. Stir in the flaked salmon and season with salt and pepper. Garnish with dill and spring onions and serve right away.

WARM ROASTED VEGETABLE SALAD

Serves 2, 4 for sharing
Prep 15 minutes
Total 35 minutes

---

225 g (8 oz/3 cups) chestnut (cremini) or button mushrooms, woody stems trimmed and quartered

2 medium sweet potatoes, unpeeled and cut into 1 cm (½ in) cubes

400 g (14 oz) Tenderstem broccoli (broccolini), rough stems trimmed and thick pieces cut lengthwise

4 shallots, trimmed and quartered through the root

90 ml (3 fl oz/⅓ cup) plus 3 tablespoons olive oil, divided

2 teaspoons ground cumin

½ teaspoon dried red chilli flakes, or more to taste

salt and freshly ground black pepper

60 g (2 oz/½ cup) pumpkin seeds

juice of 1 lemon

1 tablespoon Dijon mustard

grated Parmesan, for sprinkling

➤ Sugar snap peas, coined carrots, cauliflower, peppers and quartered red onions could be good swaps. In the spring, asparagus alone, or with green beans, are great and even better topped with a fried egg for dinner.

This is my autumn and winter go-to dinner. I end up varying the ingredients, depending on what's in season. I like roasting delicata squash as you can eat the skin (minimal prep), and I love the sweetness of it, especially when it gets nicely browned. The key to success is that everything needs to more or less cook at the same time, which also means cutting larger vegetables into smaller pieces (like the sweet potatoes). This can also be served as a delicious side dish for other dinners.

You could throw this on top of a bed of rocket (arugula), baby spinach or even quinoa, farro or something along those lines to make a grain bowl of sorts. I usually eat them as they are with the dressing, and it's more than enough for when I want to eat well and want something warming.

⏱ Make the dressing while the vegetables roast as you will have a lot of down-time. Drink or do something that makes you feel good.

Method

1. Preheat the oven to 220°C (425°F/Gas 8) with the rack in the middle of the oven.

2. On a large baking tray (sheet pan), combine the mushrooms, sweet potatoes, broccoli and shallots with 3 tablespoons of the olive oil, cumin, chilli flakes and season with salt and pepper. Use your hands to combine and coat everything well. Bake until the broccoli is charred and the sweet potatoes are lightly browned, about 20 minutes, shaking the pan and turning it around halfway to ensure even cooking. During the last 2 minutes or so of cooking, sprinkle the pumpkin seeds over to toast.

3. Meanwhile, in the bottom of a serving bowl, whisk together the lemon juice, mustard and the remaining oil, seasoning with salt and pepper as needed.

4. Scrape the vegetables into the serving bowl and toss to coat with the dressing. Finish with a generous sprinkling of cheese.

Photo on page 143

LEMONGRASS-CHICKEN
BOWL WITH RICE VERMICELLI

Serves 2, 4 for sharing
Prep 15 minutes
Total 30 minutes

5 garlic cloves, grated or minced

5 tablespoons fish sauce

2 tablespoons demerara (turbinado) sugar

6 limes, juice of 5, 1 sliced into wedges, for serving

1 lemongrass stalk, outer parts peeled and white inner parts minced or grated (page 15)

400–450 g (¾–1 lb) skinless, boneless chicken thighs, cut into 5 cm (2 in) chunks

125 ml (4¼ fl oz/½ cup) room temperature water

1 Thai bird's eye chilli (or small very hot red chilli), seeded and thinly sliced, adjusting amount based on heat preference

200 g (8 oz) packet of rice vermicelli noodles (Maifun noodles)

1 butterhead (Boston) or red leaf lettuce, leaves removed from root

½ cucumber, peeled and cut into matchsticks or shaved into thin slices

1 carrot, peeled, cut into matchsticks or shaved into thin slices

30 g (1 oz/1 cup) fresh mint, basil or coriander (cilantro) leaves and fine stems, roughly chopped

60 g (2 oz/½ cup) roasted and salted peanuts, lightly crushed (page 15)

sriracha sauce, for serving

I love that this take on the classic Vietnamese dish is basically a bowl of noodles and vegetables with some crispy meat on top. It's something I make often as the chicken char is delicious and hard to resist picking off the pan.

⏱ The key to this recipe not feeling chaotic is to prep the marinade and dipping sauce simultaneously. Set up two bowls, side by side, one for the chicken and one for the dipping sauce. Grate all the garlic at one time and divide between the bowls, and so on. Prep the veggies while the chicken is marinating and cooking.

Method

1. Preheat the grill (broiler) with the oven rack 15 cm (6 in) from the heat source (if your grill is inside your oven).

2. In a mixing bowl, combine the ingredients for the chicken marinade: 3 garlic cloves, 3 tablespoons fish sauce, 1 tablespoon sugar, juice of 2 limes and lemongrass, and mix well until the sugar is dissolved. Add the chicken and coat with the marinade. Set aside. Make the sauce with 2 garlic cloves, 2 tablespoons fish sauce, 1 tablespoon sugar, juice of 2 limes, the water and chilli. Mix until the sugar has dissolved then set aside.

3. Fill a kettle with enough water to cover the noodles and boil. Place the rice noodles in a shallow bowl and cover with the boiling water until soft and pliable, about 10 minutes or according to packet instructions. Set aside.

4. Place the chicken on a baking tray (sheet pan) and cook until the outside has started to char, about 5–7 minutes. Turn it over and cook until the chicken has reached 75°C (165°F), about 6–7 minutes more. Squeeze the juice from 1 lime over the chicken.

5. Meanwhile, drain and rinse the noodles in cold water, then leave in the same bowl to cool. Line the serving bowls with lettuce. Hand-tear them for easier-to-eat pieces or lay them whole for a prettier presentation. Place the cooled noodles inside, using (clean) kitchen scissors to cut them, and top with the cucumber, carrots, fresh herbs and peanuts then divide the chicken between bowls. Serve with sriracha, lime wedges and sauce on the side or on top.

Photo on page 118

CHARRED CORN, AVOCADO AND FETA SALAD

WITH PAN-SEARED FISH

Serves 4
Prep 10 minutes
Total 25 minutes

4 tablespoons olive oil, divided

3 sweetcorn cobs, kernels removed

½–1 jalapeño chilli, seeded and diced, depending on heat level

2 spring onions (scallions), white and light green parts, thinly sliced

salt and freshly ground pepper

4 x 175 g (6 oz) skinless fillets cod, flounder or similar white fish

juice of 2 lemons

300 g (10½ oz/2 cups) cherry tomatoes, quartered

½ teaspoon dried red chilli flakes

1 ripe Hass avocado, halved, destoned, peeled and cubed

75 g (2½ oz/½ cup) crumbled feta (preferably Bulgarian)

15 g (½ oz/½ cup) fresh basil leaves and fine stems or other herbs such as mint, coriander (cilantro) or parsley, roughly chopped

The quick-stewed tomatoes in this dish are a trick from my dad. He cooks cherry or campari tomatoes at high heat with a little salt, pepper and chilli flakes and they taste unbelievably rich with an addictive sweetness for the short amount of time they cook (I also tend to clean out the bottom of this pan with bread). Use this for fish or chicken and definitely try it with scrambled eggs.

Prep the corn, chilli, spring onions and tomato. Set the table, open the wine and do your things before you start cooking as you'll be ready to eat pretty quickly once you start.

Method

1. Heat 1 tablespoon oil in a 30 cm (12 in) frying pan (skillet) over a medium-high heat until shimmering. Add the corn, chilli, spring onions and a pinch of salt, stirring occasionally until the corn is lightly charred and the chilli softens, about 6 minutes. Set aside in a serving bowl.

2. Put the same frying pan over a medium heat and, without wiping it out, add 2 tablespoons of the oil until shimmering. Season both sides of the fish generously with salt and pepper, add to the pan skinned-side up, cooking until it easily releases without any resistance, about 3 minutes. Flip using a sturdy spatula and cook until an opaque white layer has formed at the bottom of the fish, about 1 minute more, depending on the thickness of the fish. Finish with the juice of 1 lemon and place on serving plates tented with kitchen foil.

3. Put the same frying pan over a medium heat and, without wiping it out, add a tablespoon of the oil, the tomatoes, dried chilli flakes, salt and pepper. Cook, stirring occasionally, until the tomatoes start to break down and blister, scraping up any brown bits on the bottom of the frying pan, about 3 minutes.

4. While the tomatoes are cooking, add the avocado, feta, basil, salt, pepper and juice of 1 lemon to the corn mixture. Mix to combine and adjust the seasoning as needed. Spoon the tomatoes over the fish and serve with the salad on the side.

Photo overleaf

SALAD FOR DINNER

CHARRED LETTUCE
WITH PRAWNS AND FETA DRESSING

Serves 4
Prep 5 minutes
Total 20 minutes

---

75 g (2½ oz/½ cup) crumbled feta
(preferably Bulgarian)

¼ teaspoon dried red chilli flakes

juice of 2 lemons

1 spring onion (scallion), white and light
green parts only, thinly sliced

salt and freshly ground black pepper

3 tablespoons extra-virgin olive oil

8 little gem lettuces, brown leaves
removed, sliced in half lengthwise

2 tablespoons olive oil, plus more for
coating and cooking the lettuce

12 peeled prawns (shrimp), deveined
(about 450 g/1 lb)

½ teaspoon smoked paprika

½ teaspoon ground cumin

15 g (½ oz/½ cup) fresh coriander
(cilantro) leaves and fine stems,
roughly chopped

30 g (1 oz/¼ cup) toasted pumpkin
seeds (page 15)

1 fresno or jalapeño chilli, seeded and
thinly sliced into coins (optional)

---

i Leave the core of the lettuce in tact,
so it says together during cooking.

➤ You can substitute 2 of the little
gems for 1 head of Romaine. Each
person would get 2 halves of the
Romaine instead of 4 halves of the
little gems as it's much larger – sorry
to make you do maths!

There's feta **IN THE DRESSING. Do I really need to say more than that? Okay, fine. Not only is the dressing awesome, but there's something about the taste of charred lettuce and the warmth of the wilted leaves that just does it for me. It also feels like a good way to eat salad during the winter months when it's so cold out – this is not to say that you can't have it the summer, too.**

Method

1. In a mixing bowl, combine the feta, chilli flakes, juice of 1 lemon, spring onions, pepper and extra-virgin olive oil, whisking to combine. Salt isn't needed as the feta is already quite salty from the brine, but you can season to taste.

2. Lightly rub the lettuce halves all over with olive oil and season with salt and pepper. Heat 1 teaspoon of the oil in a 30 cm (12 in) frying pan (skillet) over a medium heat until shimmering. Then add the lettuce leaves, cut-side down, working in batches, if necessary, and adding 1 teaspoon of oil each time. Cook until lightly browned in the centre with the leaves getting a darker green hue, about 3 minutes. Turn over and cook until the other side is lightly browned and wilted, about 1–2 minutes more. Set aside on serving plates, cut-side up.

3. In the same frying pan without wiping it out, heat 2 tablespoons of the oil over a medium-high heat until shimmering. Coat the prawns with the spices, season with salt and pepper and add to the frying pan. Cook until the prawns are pink all over and opaque, turning over halfway, about 4 minutes total.

4. Pour the dressing over the cut lettuce leaves, then top with the coriander, pumpkin seeds and chilli if using, plating the prawns last.

Photo overleaf

WARM FARRO SALAD

WITH ASPARAGUS, PEAS, LEAFY GREENS AND FETA

Serves 2, 4 for sharing
Prep 5 minutes
Total 45 minutes

6 tablespoons olive oil, divided

250 g (9 oz) asparagus, ends trimmed and cut into 2.5 cm (1 in) pieces (about 2 cups)

½ teaspoon dried red chilli flakes, or more as desired

salt and freshly ground black pepper

225 g (8 oz/1 cup) farro

960 ml (32 fl oz/4 cups) low-salt vegetable stock (broth) or water

juice of 1 lemon

1 tablespoon Dijon mustard

225 g (8 oz/1 cup) fresh or frozen peas

300 g (10½ oz) curly kale, cavolo nero (lacinato kale) or other leafy green, leaves removed from the stems, cut into 5 cm (2 in) ribbons (about 3 cups)

60 g (2 oz/¼ cup) flaked almonds, toasted (page 15)

4 spring onions (scallions) thinly sliced, white and light green parts only

75 g (2½ oz/½ cup) crumbled feta (preferably Bulgarian)

15 g (½ oz/½ cup) fresh coriander (cilantro) or parsley leaves and fine stems, roughly chopped

/ Look for quick-cooking farro to reduce the cooking time.

Whether visiting my sister, for work or pleasure, I've been lucky to enjoy some long stints in Paris over the years. This is great for many reasons, notably that the French are people who pride themselves on both the production and quality of food and drink and their enjoyment of it – things that I strongly align with.

This lemon-mustard dressing is my nod to the classic French mustard vinaigrette found on many bistro salads, while the nutty farro (pronounced far-o, much like my last name) is wonderful served warm as it absorbs the dressing, so each bite is tastier than the last.

⏱ You will have a good amount of downtime when the farro is cooking, so use that to prep the kale and herbs, make the dressing, clean the kitchen and set the table. And definitely pour yourself a glass of wine (maybe a French one).

Method

1. Heat 2 tablespoons olive oil in a 30 cm (12 in) frying pan (skillet) over a medium heat until shimmering. Add most of the asparagus (reserving a small amount), chilli flakes, salt and pepper. Then cook, stirring occasionally, until lightly browned, about 4 minutes. Set aside in a small bowl.

2. In the same frying pan without wiping it out, add the farro, stock and a generous amount of salt, cover and raise the heat to bring to an active boil, then lower the heat to maintain an active simmer. Cook, keeping it covered, until the farro is tender and not chewy, about 30 minutes (add water if necessary to keep the farro covered). Check on it every 10 minutes or so to make sure it's simmering and nothing is sticking to the bottom.

3. While the farro is cooking, in a serving bowl, whisk the lemon juice, mustard and 4 tablespoons of the oil. Season with salt and pepper.

4. Drain the farro and transfer to the bowl with the dressing. Toss to combine, then stir in peas, cooked and raw asparagus and kale. Let stand until peas are tender and kale is wilted, about 5 minutes. Mix in almonds, spring onions, feta and coriander. Season as needed.

CUMIN-SPICED STEAK SALAD
WITH AVOCADO AND KALE

Serves 2, 4 for sharing
Prep 5 minutes
Total 25 minutes

2 x 175 g (6 oz) skirt or flank steaks, cut across the width of the steak into 13 cm (5 in) pieces

salt and freshly ground black pepper

1 tablespoon ground cumin

300 g (10½ oz) cavolo nero (lacinato kale), curly kale or other leafy green, leaves removed from the stems, cut into 5 cm (2 in) ribbons (about 3 cups)

¼ teaspoon dried red chilli flakes or more as desired

juice of 1 lemon

2 ripe Hass avocados, halved, destoned peeled and cubed

1 tablespoon ghee or 2 tablespoons rapeseed (canola) oil

30 g (1 oz/¼ cup) toasted pumpkin seeds (page 15)

15 g (½ oz/½ cup) coriander (cilantro) or parsley leaves and fine stems, roughly chopped or torn

/ Massaging and cutting the kale helps to tenderise it, and rids it of that rough and thick texture. The longer it sits with the avocado, the tastier it is, and it makes for great leftovers.

Use leftover steak for the Skirt steak tacos (page 165), or one one of the other salads in this section.

This is one of those salads that I make over and over again, sometimes changing it up to add in a bit of feta or different proteins on top, which I highly encourage you to do as well. My good friend Katie, a talented and brilliant chef, first taught me a version of this with mango many years ago, and it's evolved into this. I get lazy and usually tear the kale with my hands, but, the finer you chop it, the airier and lighter it will be.

Cumin happens to be one of my favourite spices; I put it on almost everything I make, from sprinkling some into my scrambled eggs to dousing roasted vegetables with it. If you, for some unknown reason, don't share my love of it, then reduce the amount as it is quite strong in this particular recipe.

Method

1. Generously season the steak with salt, pepper and half the cumin, making sure to get it in all the cracks and crevices. Set aside at room temperature while you make the salad.

2. In a serving bowl, mix the kale, remaining cumin, chilli flakes, lemon juice, half the avocado and season with salt and pepper. Use your hands to massage the avocado and spices into the kale, making sure it's well coated. You can be rough and tough with this one, as there's nothing delicate going on here. And it's a good way to take out any residual aggression from the day.

3. Heat the ghee in a 30 cm (12 in) frying pan over a medium-high heat until melted/lightly smoking. Add the steak in one layer, working in batches if needed, turning over after 3 minutes, and cooking until an instant-read thermometer reaches 52°C (125°F) for medium rare and 57°C (135°F) for medium, about 6 minutes total for medium rare. (If you feel like the steaks are charring too quickly, then continuously flip them until they finish cooking.) Set aside on a cutting board and let rest for 5–10 minutes while you set the table and pour yourself some wine.

4. Portion the salad onto serving plates, add the remaining avocado cubes, topping them with pumpkin seeds and coriander. Season the steak with a sprinkle of salt, slice against the grain, and distribute on the salad plates, finishing with pepper.

SCOTS, WHISKY AND SCALLOPS

Over the years, as a food and travel writer, I've found myself in some surreal (but nice) situations that I would otherwise unlikely to be in. Take, for example, the time I was at *Food & Wine* magazine and watched two famed chefs have an impromptu pizza showdown, which resulted in one of them shaving truffles on the pizza with abandon – like Salt Bae going at it, but with incredibly expensive truffles. Or, times that I've found myself eating Michelin-starred, three-hour dinners solo around the world – and getting paid to do it.

Or, the time I spent an afternoon with a tall, handsome Scottish chef, donning a kilt and teaching me about seafood and whisky. He's charming, funny and, obviously, as an American, I'm a sucker for anyone who doesn't have a flat American accent. The mystery man is Michael Smith, the chef/owner of Loch Bay on the Isle of Skye, which has recently been awarded a Michelin star (way to go!). He was there promoting Scottish tourism, namely seafood and whisky for our purposes. He regaled me with tales of cooks diving for sea urchin during their breaks, the incredible seafood that sits outside his door and the beauty of the Scottish highlands. I ate it right up. Like a moth to a flame.

But, most importantly, he taught me a foolproof way to cook scallops that I will be eternally grateful for. And now, I share it with you. My apologies for not being a dashing Scotsman.

When you're using high-quality scallops (as you should), you don't actually want them to be cooked all the way through; kind of like eating a medium rare steak. In this method, the scallops end up being perfectly cooked, and by that I mean the centre is medium rare. If this is making you squeamish, a) it's not a terrible idea to get over it and b) you can cook them for a minute longer. It's also a foolproof way to avoid overcooking scallops, which then acquire a rubbery and unpleasant texture.

Here's what you do: Heat a pan over a medium-high heat with your cooking fat of choice until lightly smoking. Season the scallops with salt and pepper and add them to the pan. Do not move them! Avoid the temptation to poke around and lift them as you want them to get a nice brown crust. Instead, watch the side of the scallop to see when it changes from a murky pinkish-white colour to more of a creamy, pearl white. When the colour is about halfway up the scallop (or about 3 minutes later), use metal tongs or a spatula to flip them. If one of the scallops gives you some resistance and feels like it's tugging to remain on the pan, then let it sit for a few seconds longer until it easily releases. Leave on the heat for about 1 minute more, then remove from the stove and let the residual heat from the pan finish cooking the scallops for 1–2 minutes more. Use this time to finish any last-minute plating, such as putting herbs or dressings on, and then add a squeeze of lemon and divvy up the scallops to eat promptly.

Thank you, Michael!

FUN FACTS

In the UK, and many other parts of the world, scallops are sold in their shell. Aren't they pretty?

The scallop muscle is the tiny bump that sticks out from the rest of the meat, like a callous or something funky attached itself to the scallop. It can easily be pulled off, as it will take on a rubbery texture when cooked. No biggie if you forget though.

SCALLOP AND BRUSSELS SPROUT SALAD

WITH VEGAN CAESAR DRESSING

Serves 4
Prep 10 minutes
Total 20 minutes

1 garlic clove, grated or mashed with the back of a knife until it's paste-like

1 tablespoon miso paste

1 tablespoon Dijon mustard

juice of 2 lemons

4 tablespoons extra-virgin olive oil

900 g (2 lb/6 cups) shredded Brussels sprouts

60 g (2 oz/2 cups) shop-bought croutons

salt and freshly ground black pepper

2 tablespoons olive oil

12 large scallops, muscles removed

15 g (½ oz/½ cup) fresh parsley leaves and fine stems, roughly chopped

30 g (1 oz/¼ cup) toasted pumpkin seeds (page 15)

🖊 If you can purchase shredded Brussels sprouts, then do that as a time-saver. Otherwise, use a mandolin or trim them and use a knife to cut into strips.

➤ Prawns (shrimp) or chicken work here as well.

Swap sprouts for asparagus in the spring or a mix of kale and Romaine.

This vegan dressing is a slight variation on the one from Haven's Kitchen, a fabulous cooking school, event space and café of sorts in Chelsea, NYC. I first heard about it when my sister worked there, which is how I became obsessed with its well-curated goods in the café portion and the impeccable taste of its owner (who is lovely). Definitely check it out when you're in town, and tell them I say hi. Why serve a vegan dressing with a protein? In my experience, a lot of home cooks don't want to make a dressing with anchovies and raw eggs (yes, that's in a Caesar, in case you didn't know). Plus, it feels a little lighter, and I'm into that.

Method

1. In the bottom of a large serving bowl, combine the garlic, miso paste, mustard and juice of 1 lemon. Slowly pour in the extra-virgin olive oil, whisking at intervals to combine it with the ingredients. Make sure to mash and break up the miso paste, and continue until it reaches a smoothish consistency. (It's not going to be perfect as we're doing it by hand, but you could use a hand-held blender if you'd like.) Add water or more lemon juice to thin out until you achieve your desired consistency and taste. Mix in the Brussels sprouts and croutons until thoroughly combined. Season with salt and pepper and set aside.

2. In a 30 cm (12 in) frying pan (skillet) over a medium-high heat, add the remaining 2 tablespoons olive oil and heat until lightly smoking. Season the scallops with salt and pepper on both sides, then add to the pan, making sure they are not touching each other (work in batches if you need to). Cook until about halfway up the scallop is opaque and more of a creamy white colour than a murky white, about 3 minutes. The scallops should easily release from the frying pan without resistance (keep cooking if not) and have a nice browned crust on the bottom. Flip, cooking for 1 more minute for medium-rare, then remove from the stove to allow the residual heat of the pan to finish cooking them. (If you want them fully cooked through, then leave on the heat for 1–2 minutes more.)

3. Squeeze the remaining lemon juice on them, then divide the salad between plates, top with scallops, parsley and pumpkin seeds.

CURRIED VEGAN QUINOA

WITH BROCCOLI AND LEMON-TAHINI DRESSING

Serves 2, 4 for sharing
Prep 5 minutes
Total 25 minutes

---

6 tablespoons olive oil, divided

1 teaspoon curry powder, or more, depending on preference

½ teaspoon ground cumin

3–4 small broccoli stalks, stems trimmed and cut into bite-sized pieces (about 4 cups)

salt and freshly ground black pepper

200 g (7 oz/1 cup) quinoa, rinsed

500 ml (17 fl oz/2 cups) low-salt vegetable stock (broth) or water

1 tablespoon tahini

juice of 1 lemon

300 g (10½ oz) cavolo nero (lacinato kale), curly kale or other leafy green, leaves removed from the stems, cut into 5 cm (2 in) ribbons (about 3 cups)

15 g (½ oz/½ cup) fresh coriander (cilantro) or flat leaf parsley, leaves and fine stems, roughly chopped

Pickled red onions (page 54)

✎ The broccoli should be cut into bite-sized pieces so it cooks quickly.

▥ Use leftover Pickled red onions for the Charred steak with corn tacos, (page 165) and Sleeveless sweet potato jackets (page 44). They will last up to a week in an airtight container in the fridge.

I'll always have a soft spot for Santa Monica, LA for several reasons, but what I love most is that you can be active outside and eat well, all the time – two of my favourite things. Plus, the weather and produce are almost always fantastic. This health bowl is my ode to vegetable-filled eating.

⏱ Make the Pickled red onions. Prep the broccoli, then start cooking, and chop the kale while the quinoa is cooking. Use the quinoa cooking time to make the dressing, clean up the kitchen and set the table.

Method

1. Heat 2 tablespoons of the oil, curry powder and cumin in a 30 cm (12 in) frying pan (skillet) with a tight-fitting lid over a medium-high heat until shimmering. Add the broccoli and season with salt and pepper. Cook, stirring occasionally, until lightly browned and just tender, about 6–7 minutes. Remove from the frying pan and set aside.

2. In the same frying pan without wiping it out, lower the heat to medium and add the quinoa and let it toast until it is fragrant, about 1 minute.

3. Add the stock and a little salt, cover and raise the heat to reach and maintain an active boil. Keep covered and cook until the quinoa is soft with the spirals open, about 9 minutes.

4. While the quinoa is cooking, make the dressing. In the bottom of a serving bowl, mix the tahini, juice of 1 lemon and 4 tablespoons of the oil. Season to taste with salt.

5. When the quinoa is finished, reduce the heat to low, stir in the kale and broccoli, until the kale is wilted, about 2 minutes more. Season to taste with salt and pepper. Pour the quinoa into the bowl, mix well to coat with the dressing, then top with the coriander and pickled red onions and serve. Alternatively, if your cookware is beautiful, pour the dressing into the pot, stir to combine and serve.

GARLICKY ROMAINE

SUMMER SALAD

Serves 2, 4 for sharing
Prep 15 minutes
Total 15 minutes

---

juice of 2 lemons

2 garlic cloves, grated or mashed into a paste

2 tablespoons extra-virgin olive oil

salt and freshly ground black pepper

1 Romaine lettuce, tough outer leaves discarded, cut into 5 cm (2 in) ribbons

½ red onion, thinly sliced

150 g (5 oz/1 cup) baby plum (grape) tomatoes, halved

1 cucumber, peeled and cut into half moons

75 g (2½ oz/½ cup) crumbled feta (preferably Bulgarian), plus extra to serve

1 Hass avocado, halved, destoned, peeled and sliced

15 g (½ oz/½ cup) fresh mint leaves and fine stems, roughly chopped, plus more for sprinkling

crusty bread, to serve

For simply cooked chicken breasts:
Preheat the grill (broiler) with the pan 15 cm (6 in) from the heat source (if it's located inside of your oven). Coat 4 skinless, boneless chicken breasts with 2 tablespoons of olive oil, 1 teaspoon dried oregano (optional) and season with salt and pepper. Place on a baking tray (sheet pan) and grill until lightly browned, about 5–7 minutes. Take out the tray, flip and grill until the chicken is cooked through, about 5–7 minutes.

My dad makes this recipe in the summer, and, when the salad is done, he usually passes me the bowl and says, 'go on, you can drink it, I know you want to'. And I do, when it's just the two of us. The garlicky, tomato-juice-filled liquid, sprinkled with dissolved bits of feta, is basically my idea of heaven. After slurping it down, I always take a piece of bread and wipe it clean. You would not be wrong if you judged me right now, but, man, it is so good.

This is the kind of salad dressing that leaves a strong, pungent garlic taste in your mouth for a few hours after you eat it. Basically, you need to make sure that everyone you're with also eats it and then be on a 24-hour watch of your breath. You also have to love garlic. I crave making this on hot summer days when it feels wrong to eat anything other than chilled foods and when I see really beautiful, crisp Romaine.

This is a perfect salad to use with the other proteins in this chapter, like scallops, prawns (shrimp), grilled (broiled) chicken or steak. It's also fantastic left as a vegetarian option during hot summer months, which is exactly how I eat it. If you have leftover cucumbers, for any reason, slice them and top with good quality salt as a snack (one of my faves).

Method

1. In the bottom of the serving bowl, whisk together the lemon juice, garlic, oil, salt and pepper until combined. Toss in the lettuce, red onion, tomatoes, cucumber and feta, mixing to combine until all the leaves are coated well. (You can go ahead and try a piece to make sure.) Top with the avocado and mint. Serve with bread.

LOOK MORE IMPRESSIVE THAN THEY ARE

Go-to roast chicken (page 146) and Warm roasted
vegetable salad (page 126)

ME &

This was one of many names I threw out for this cookbook, and, in fairness, I get why it didn't work as it doesn't capture the essence of this book, but, in some ways, it does of this chapter. When I began telling friends that I was writing my first cookbook, the immediate reactions were, 'wow, that's so exciting! How glamorous'. And it totally is exciting and feels like such a wowing thing, but, in reality, it's me in my pjs at home, clacking away on the computer and testing and re-testing recipes in my kitchen. There's really nothing glamorous about it, especially if you were to hoverboard up to my window and look in.

What also inevitably pops up in the same conversation is being asked what my favourite recipe is, and my answer is, well, I love the ones that I throw together quickly that both look and taste more impressive than they are. And, while it is the name of this chapter, I actually feel like it extends to most of this book – these are all recipes that make me feel good and proud of myself for getting my sh*t together and cooking something fab, even if I'm the only one who secretly knows how easy it was (and now you know, too...).

MY PJS

Here, you'll find some recipes that look like restaurant-style dishes but come together in just 20 minutes, like the Ginger-curried lamb chops with braised greens (page 162), while a few are on the longer side like the Go-to roast chicken (page 146) – still under an hour. Others might seem out of your skill set, like the Roasted whole fish (page 155), but I promise you that they are not. Just picture me with you in the kitchen (in nice clothes with clean hair and make-up, preferably), sipping on some wine and saying lots of encouraging words, because I know you can do this. And, even if you mess up a little, and it's not quite as pretty as you'd like, then you'll ace it the next time. Promise.

GO-TO ROAST CHICKEN

Serves 2, 4 for sharing
Prep 5 minutes
Total 50 minutes

---

1 x 1.5–1.8 kg (3½–4 lb) chicken, spatchcocked (page 147)

salt and freshly ground black pepper

1 lemon, halved through the belly

3 tablespoons olive oil

450 g (1 lb) baby potatoes, halved

30 g (1 oz/1 cup) flat leaf parsley, leaves and fine stems, roughly chopped

fresh thyme sprigs (optional)

30 g (1 oz/1 cup) mixed fresh herbs of your choice, such as coriander (cilantro), thyme or basil, leaves and fines stems, roughly chopped

2 tablespoons drained capers, roughly chopped

4 spring onions (scallions), white and light green parts only, thinly sliced

½ teaspoon dried red chilli flakes (optional)

juice of ½ lemon, or more to taste

120 ml (4 fl oz/½ cup) extra-virgin olive oil

✏ For crispy skin, it's crucial that the chicken is dry when you put it in the oven, aka no water moisture. Pat it dry with paper towels to absorb any moisture before seasoning it.

🗄 Save remaining salsa verde as it can be kept overnight in an airtight container in the fridge. It's great with the eggs or the Simple whole fish (page 155).

My favourite part of this recipe is the chicken fat-infused potatoes that get a hint of lemon as they roast, so you get crispy, creamy and lemony potatoes that go perfectly with tender, juicy chicken.

Method

1. Preheat the oven to 230°C (430°F/Gas 8) with a rack in the middle and one 15 cm (6 in) from the heat source. Place a roasting tin in the oven to heat. Dry the chicken with paper towels and season the chicken with salt and pepper. Make sure to get it all over. If it doesn't make you too squeamish, then lift up the skin of the breast area and gently use your fingers to loosen it, creating a little pocket to wiggle your fingers into. Be careful not to tear a hole the skin. Do the same with the thigh area. Add salt and pepper in that little space with fresh thyme sprigs, if using. If you can prepare the chicken the night before, you can do this then, which is even better.

2. Place the chicken skin-side up in the centre of the tray. Lightly rub 1 tablespoon olive oil all over, making sure not to burn your hands. Nestle the lemon halves in there, cut-side down.

3. Roast until the skin just starts to brown, about 20 minutes. Meanwhile, toss the potatoes with 2 tablespoons olive oil and season with salt and pepper. Remove the chicken and flip over using tongs and a wooden spoon to help guide it without tearing the skin. Spread the potatoes around the chicken in an even layer. Cook for another 15 minutes, then remove and flip again for the last 5–10 minutes of cooking, pushing the potatoes around. The chicken is done when the juices run clear when pierced with a fork or an instant-read thermometer reaches 75°C (165°F) in the thigh, away from the bone. Let the chicken rest for 5–10 minutes, while you set the table and refresh wine glasses. If the chicken skin is not as browned as you'd like, then turn on the grill (broiler) and grill the chicken for 2–4 minutes, depending on your grill, until the skin is crispy.

4. Meanwhile, prepare the salsa verde. In a serving bowl, combine the parsley, other fresh herbs, capers, spring onions, chilli flakes, lemon juice and extra-virgin olive oil. Season with salt and pepper.

5. When the chicken is done, squeeze the charred lemon halves over it, garnish with the salsa verde, and serve the remainder on the table along with the potatoes.

Photo on page 146

LOOK MORE IMPRESSIVE THAN THEY ARE

WINNER, WINNER, CHICKEN DINNER

This is one of my favourite phrases of all time, and I'm really happy my lovely editor let me put it in somewhere (the other, in case you were curious, is 'easy peasy, lemon squeezy' which I tried to make the subtitle of this book). In my efforts to become a better home cook, I felt like I needed to nail a solid roast chicken recipe. I mean, what's better during winter than a comforting plate of roast chicken and potatoes? Especially on a lazy Sunday when you're staying inside all day. Yet, it can be intimidating – how do you get crispy skin and juicy meat? How do I not overcook this thing?

So, I did what I do best: I ate and read. This recipe came about as a combination between two of my favourite chicken recipes, that of the late Judy Rodgers of Zuni Café in San Francisco and the chicken at Barbuto, a restaurant that was in NYC's West Village run by Jonathan Waxman.

Rodgers pre-salts a whole chicken up to 24 hours ahead, and uses a smaller-sized bird as they brown more easily at high heat. She turns her chicken twice during the cooking process and famously serves hers with a bread salad. Waxman, on the other hand, serves his with a salsa verde, and spatchcocks his small bird, then cuts it in half and cooks the two pieces at high heat on a metal plate in an extremely hot oven.

I played around with their recipes and others, and this is where I ended up.

For the two whole chicken recipes, I spatchcock the chicken so it cooks faster and more evenly, salt it, cook it at a high heat and turn twice during the cooking process. At the same time, I surround the bird with potatoes so that anything that cooks off the chicken is soaked up by them and makes them all crazy delicious.

Spatchcocking is such a fun word
First piece of advice – ask your butcher to do it for you. They usually will if you ask, though you might have to say it's removing the backbone as not everyone loves/ is as familiar with this word. (It's basically butterflying it, but spatchocking sounds way more fun.)

How to do it: This can seem a little intimidating the first time, but, once you get the hang of it, it's actually quite easy. Use kitchen scissors to remove the back bone by cutting closely along it on both sides. At first, I was always afraid that I'd end up cutting up half the chicken. I did not, and neither will you.

Lay it breast-side up, then, using your palms, press down to crack the breast bone so that it actually flattens. (This is kind of the whoa part, and, also quite fun, after you do it a few times.)

HARISSA-GHEE ROAST CHICKEN

Serves 2, 4 for sharing
Prep 5 minutes
Total 50 minutes

---

4 tablespoons ghee

1 x 1.5–1.8 kg (3½–4 lb) chicken, spatchcocked (page 147)

salt and freshly ground black pepper

1 teaspoon ground cumin

1 orange, halved through the belly

2 tablespoons harissa

250 g (9 oz/1 cup) thick yoghurt, such as Greek or skyr

½ large cucumber, peeled and diced or grated and juices drained

30 g (1 oz/1 cup) fresh parsley or coriander (cilantro) leaves and fine stems, roughly chopped

extra-virgin olive oil, for drizzling

Grate the cucumber over a bowl and drain the liquid so that it doesn't make the yoghurt too loose. Diced will give you more of a chunky yoghurt. (Both are fab.)

Add potatoes like we do in the Spatchcocked chicken recipe (page 146)

This makes delicious sandwiches with leftover chicken, yoghurt and fresh herbs.

Look at you spatchcocking left and right! Making me so proud. There are no side vegetables in this recipe, so you can serve it with one of the Salad for dinner recipes, like the Garlicky romaine summer salad (page 141).

Method

1. Preheat the oven to 230°C (450°F/Gas 8) with a rack in the middle and one 15 cm (6 in) from the heat source. Place the roasting tin in the oven to heat. At the same time, place a ramekin with the ghee in the oven until warm and melted. (This will happen fairly quickly so keep an eye on it.)

2. Dry the chicken with paper towels and season with salt and pepper all over. If it doesn't make you too squeamish, then lift up the skin of the breast area and gently use your fingers to loosen it, creating a little pocket to wiggle your fingers into, without tearing a hole the skin. Do the same with the thigh area. Add salt and pepper in that little space. If you can prepare the chicken the night before, then you can do this then, which is even better. Place the chicken in a roasting tin. Pour the ghee over the chicken, making sure to also coat the underside of it as well and not burn yourself. Place the orange halves next to it, cut-side down.

3. Roast until the skin just starts to brown, about 20 minutes. Remove the chicken and flip over using tongs and a wooden spoon to help guide it without tearing the skin. If there is any liquid in the pan, then use a spoon to baste the chicken with it before you flip it over and after. Cook for another 15 minutes, then remove and flip again, basting with any liquid and carefully rubbing the harissa over both sides of the chicken, and cook for 5–10 minutes more. The chicken is done when the juices run clear when pierced with a fork or an instant-read thermometer reaches 75°C (165°F) in the thigh, away from the bone. If the chicken skin is not as browned as you'd like, then turn on the grill (broiler) and cook for 2–4 minutes, depending on the heat of your broiler, until the skin is crispy.

4. Let the chicken rest for 5–10 minutes in a warm spot (and give it a good coating with any juices), while you set the table, refresh wine glasses and make the yoghurt. In a serving bowl, mix the yoghurt with the cucumber, half the parsley, a little salt and a drizzle of extra-virgin olive oil.

5. Squeeze one of the orange halves on top of the chicken, top with parsley and serve with the yoghurt and salad.

PROSCIUTTO-WRAPPED COD WITH GARLICKY SPINACH

Serves 4
Prep 10 minutes
Total 25 minutes

---

4 x 175 g (6 oz) white fish fillets about
    4 cm (1½ in) thick, such as cod, hake,
    flounder or haddock

salt and freshly ground black pepper

8 very thin slices prosciutto

3 tablespoons olive oil, divided

1 medium shallot, thinly sliced

½ teaspoon of dried red chilli flakes,
    or more as desired

2 garlic cloves, grated or minced

3 tablespoons low-salt chicken
    stock (broth)

400 g (15 oz) tin cannellini beans,
    drained and rinsed

125 g (4 oz/2 packed cups) baby spinach
    or other quick-cooking leafy greens

2 lemons, 1 for juice, 1 sliced into
    wedges, for serving

Fish seems to be something that home cooks don't always love making, even though it's delicious, quick and so good for you.

Enter this recipe: it's crispy, crunchy and foolproof. The prosciutto seals in the flavour and infuses the fish with a delicious saltiness; plus, it helps to stop the fish from overcooking and sticking to the pan. Pair it with some simply cooked greens and some wine and it will feel like you've got life figured out at this moment.

⏱ Prep the shallot, beans and garlic so you can devote your attention to the fish (especially the first time you make the recipe). When you feel confident with this method, then prep these as the fish cooks.

Method

1. Season the cod with salt and pepper. Wrap 2 slices of prosciutto around the middle of each cod fillet – more like a jacket than a sleeping bag – overlapping them slightly at the top and bottom.

2. In a cast iron pan or large heavy-weight frying pan (skillet), heat 2 tablespoons of the oil over a medium-high heat until shimmering. Add the fillets, seam-side down (you want the seams to get contact with the pan so that they seal together), and cook until the prosciutto is crispy on the bottom side, about 3–4 minutes. Flip the fillets and cook until the second side is crispy, about 3–4 minutes longer (reduce the heat if the cod or prosciutto threatens to burn). The unwrapped pieces of fish will look like they are ready to flake and start to separate slightly. Transfer the fish to a paper towel-lined plate, cover loosely with foil, and set aside.

3. Add the remaining tablespoon of the oil to the pan, without wiping it out, reducing to a medium heat. Add the shallot with a little salt and cook until softened, about 2 minutes. Add the chilli flakes and garlic, stirring constantly until fragrant, about 30 seconds. Add the stock, scraping up any brown bits on the bottom with a wooden spoon, then stir in the beans and spinach. Cook until the beans are soft and the liquid has been absorbed, about 3 minutes. Off the heat, stir in the lemon juice and adjust the seasoning with salt and pepper. Serve with the cod and lemon wedges on the side.

    LOOK MORE IMPRESSIVE THAN THEY ARE

PORK CHOPS
WITH NECTARINES AND A KICK

Serves 2
Prep 5 minutes
Total 25 minutes

---

2 x 4 cm (1½ in) thick bone-in rib or centre-cut pork chops with the fat cap, if it has one (about 275 g/ 10 oz each)

salt and freshly ground black pepper

1 tablespoon olive oil

3 nectarines, peaches or plums, stoned and cut into 1 cm (½ in) slices

zest and juice of 1 lemon

1 teaspoon demerera (turbinado) sugar

½ teaspoon dried red chilli flakes

60 g (2 oz/1 cup) rocket (arugula) or baby spinach

extra-virgin olive oil, for rocket

1 tablespoon ghee

15 g (½ oz/½ cup) fresh basil leaves and fine stems, roughly chopped, for sprinkling

---

*When cooking or grilling stone fruit, buy ones that are harder than you typically would eat so that they hold together during the cooking process. They should be firm without any give. Side note: if you have not yet grilled stone fruit in the summer and served them with ice cream or grilled cookies, put that at the top of your to-do list. You can thank me later.

The pork is almost an afterthought as it's really the stone fruit and sauce that make this dish special: sweet, spicy and slightly charred nectarines feel like an embodiment of all that is great about summer – pair with a chilled glass of wine and a water view, and we are talking dreams coming true.

⏱ Cut the fruit while the pork chops are cooking as well as getting the zest, sugar and basil ready, as it moves quickly once the pork chops are done.

Method

1. Season the pork chops generously with salt and pepper. Heat 1 tablespoon olive oil in a cast iron pan or other heavy frying pan (skillet) over medium-high heat until glistening and the pan seems scary hot. Add the pork chops and cook without moving until the first side has a nice brown crust, about 5–7 minutes (you can take a peek under when you start to see the sides have started to brown, if you're getting nervous.) Use tongs to flip, allowing the other side to brown for a minute, then flip continuously, every 30 seconds, using a spoon to coat it with pan juices, until the internal temperature registers 62°C (145°F) on a meat thermometer for medium rare, about 5–7 minutes total (cooking time will depend on how thick your pork chops are and will be reduced if much thinner). Transfer to a plate, cover loosely with foil and let them rest as they will continue to cook while you make the nectarines and sauce.

2. Without wiping out the frying pan, reduce the heat to medium-low and add the nectarines, lemon zest, sugar, chilli flakes and a pinch of salt. Stir gently until the nectarines begin to soften but don't lose their shape, about 2–3 minutes.

3. Meanwhile, divide the rocket between two plates, dress with oil and salt. Add the pork chops to the serving plates and pour any remaining juices back into the pan with the nectarines, stirring in the ghee and lemon juice. Use a wooden spoon to scrape up any browned bits from the bottom of the pan, swirling it around until ghee is melted and creates a thick, congealed sauce, about 2–3 minutes more. Season to taste with salt and pepper. Stir in half of the basil. Divide the nectarines between the plates, spoon the sauce on top and sprinkle with the remaining basil. Serve immediately.

LOOK MORE IMPRESSIVE THAN THEY ARE

DON'T LET A WHOLE FISH SCARE YOU

One day, when my sister and I were walking on a 'busy' street high above the water in Santorini about 10 years ago, the wind forcefully blew up our skirts, lifting them high in the air. As we panicked, trying to slap down both the front and backs and still hobble forward, an old man with tanned, weathered skin riding a donkey passed by, winked at us and said, 'Let it free my ba-bieeees' and continued on. While we did not heed his advice regarding our skirts, that phrase has stuck with us over the years and we use it often, whether it's when we are hesitant about trying something new or are out of our comfort zones.

I do think there is something to be said about working hard then letting go and trusting that it will all work out in one way or another, rather than worrying so much about the outcome (I'm saying this to myself as much as you). Plus, as Baz Luhrmann so eloquently said, 'worrying is as effective as chewing bubble gum to solve an algebra problem'. This all can be applied to something as simple as this recipe.

Cooking a whole fish seems intimidating: how do I know when it's done? Will I overcook it? How on earth do I fillet it like they do in restaurants? Maybe the eyes freak you out. Well, I think you've got to abandon all fear and tackle it, trusting that whether it works out perfectly or not, you've done it. Hey, this can be that thing you do today that scares you.

Once you get the hang of the technique, which is pretty easy as the fish are placed on lemon slices so it doesn't stick to the tray, you realise that you're simply putting it in the oven, making your side pieces and creating a gorgeous, good-for-you meal. Deboning the fish is the complicated part, but I promise if you follow those simple steps, with a little practise, you can do it. (Maybe don't invite people over the first couple of times you try it.)

How to debone a roasted fish

First, remove the stuffing and anything left on the bottom of the pan (these can be used to garnish the serving plate). Use a spoon and fork to cradle the head, then lift it up towards the body until it snaps off. Then, cut off the tail using the same snapping method. Move the fish to one side of the tray so you have some space to work with.

Cut off the fin bones from the back of the fish (the still closed side of the fish, which you are basically scraping off so it looks like the other side). They should easily come off, which means that it's cooked. Then, use the spoon to scrape away the belly meat on the other side of the cavity, repeating much the same action. (The belly meat will be kind of fatty and will look shinier than the actual fillet.) Then, use the spoon to gently scrape away the skin and push both the belly and skin to the discarded side of the tray. Locating the spine, which will more or less be visible or peek down the side, cut along the length of the spine, moving from one end to the other. Then use both utensils to gently remove the meat on one side off of it until it easily slides off (it's okay if the end part breaks off). Repeat with the other side – the belly side will be a little fattier, so you can pick and choose the good meat. Move all the good meat to the serving plate.

Take the tail end of the spine and lift it up towards the head so that it easily releases. Check for any remaining bones (run the back of the spoon down the fish to see if it hits anything hard as a test) then split the fish down the centre, along the spine imprint. Place the meat on the serving plate, season with some lemon and a drizzle of good extra-virgin olive oil.

Always remember, if this process feels overwhelming, then just use your hands to pick off the bits of meat and have some fun. Just don't forget to dig out the fish cheeks as they are sweet and tender.

SIMPLE WHOLE FISH
WITH CHARRED CITRUS

Serves 2
Prep 5 minutes
Total 30 minutes

4 lemons, 3 with ends trimmed and sliced thinly, juice of 1

fresh herb sprigs, such as thyme, rosemary or oregano

olive oil

salt and freshly ground black pepper

2 whole fish (450 g/1 lb each), such as trout, sea bass or branzino, scales and gills removed, scored (see recipe note) and gutted

extra-virgin olive oil, for drizzling

Score the fish: Using a paring knife, make diagonal slashes on both sides of the fish skin, about 2.5 cm (1 in) apart, moving from just below the collar to the base of the tail (see photo overleaf). It's okay if you hit the meat as it will infuse it with the seasonings.

During an island boat excursion from Santorini, we ate what can only be described as simplicity at its best: grilled octopus; a Greek salad with plump, red tomatoes, fresh, crunchy cucumbers and blocks of feta, and a simple whole grilled fish. As we devoured the meal, sitting along the water, we remarked, as I'm sure most people do in that situation, why don't we eat and live like this at home? Yes, there are several factors, namely that, while Manhattan and the UK are both islands to an extent, they are of a very different variety than Santorini.

So the next couple of recipes are for when you want a taste of holidays at home with bright and bold flavours that take you back to a loved trip or perhaps encourage you to book a new one. Serve with a side salad.

Method

1. Preheat the oven to 230°C (450°F/Gas 8) and place a baking tray (sheet pan) in the oven on the middle rack.

2. Remove the baking tray. Place the lemons in 2 rows in the middle of the tray so that they are roughly the length of the fish and so they have enough space between them so that the 2 fish don't touch when placed on top of the lemons. Place a herb sprig on top of the lemons. Generously oil and salt both sides of the fish and inside the cavities, rubbing into the slash marks. Then fill the cavity with remaining lemon and herbs, placing each fish on top of one row of lemons. Roast until the fish is opaque and easily flakes when touched with a fork and reaches 60°C (140°F) in the thickest part of the fish, typically near the spine, about 20 minutes. Let rest for 5 minutes while you set up the table and mentally prepare yourself to carve it.

3. After carving (page opposite), finish with lemon juice and a drizzle of extra-virgin olive oil. Garnish the plates with some of the lemon slices and serve. (You should eat some of these lemon slices.)

ROASTED WHOLE FISH

WITH SALSA VERDE AND LEMONY POTATOES

Serves 2
Prep 5 minutes
Total 30 minutes

Whole roasted fish (page 155)

450 g (1 lb) baby potatoes, quartered

3 tablespoons olive oil

1 teaspoon dried oregano

salt and freshly ground pepper

30 g (1¼ oz/1 packed cup) fresh parsley, leaves and fine stems, roughly chopped

30 g (1 oz/1 cup) mixed fresh herbs of your choice, such as coriander (cilantro), thyme, basil, mint or chives, roughly chopped

2 tablespoons drained capers, roughly chopped

4 spring onions (scallions), white and light green parts only, thinly sliced

½ teaspoon dried red chilli flakes (optional)

juice of 1½ lemons, divided, or more to taste

120 ml (4 fl oz/½ cup) extra-virgin olive oil

*This is the same salsa verde from the Go-to roast chicken (page 146), so if you've already made it once, then, hey, you're ahead of the game! Plus, it can be kept overnight in an airtight container in the fridge, if you want to make the chicken the next day.

One of my favourite places in Barcelona is La Paradeta, a casual seafood restaurant, where you pick out your seafood and choose how you want it cooked: razor clams, huge prawns (shrimp) and lobster tails are some of the best things to eat *a la plancha* (grilled) with a delicious herb-filled sauce drizzled on top. The room is sparse in style but full of lively, energetic people chatting away. This is my at-home version of that experience. Invite some friends over to liven it up.

Make the salsa while the fish cooks, have a glass of wine and set the table.

1. Prepare the fish on a heated baking tray (sheet pan) as instructed on page 155. Surround the fish with potatoes and dress the potatoes with 3 tablespoons olive oil, oregano and season with salt and pepper. Roast until the fish is opaque and easily flakes when touched with a fork and reaches 60°C (140°F) in the thickest part of the fish, typically near the spine, about 20 minutes. Let rest for 5 minutes while you set up the table and mentally prepare yourself to carve it.

2. While the fish is cooking, make the salsa verde. In a serving bowl, combine the parsley, other fresh herbs, capers, spring onions, chilli flakes, juice of ½ a lemon or more to taste and extra-virgin olive oil. Season with salt and pepper.

3. Squeeze the juice of 1 lemon over the potatoes and juice of 1 lemon over the fish before serving. Divide between plates.

Yay, you did it! Way to go. Please send me a photo, no matter how ugly or pretty you think it is. I think you did just great.

For different sides, use 2 navel oranges instead of lemons, layering the orange slices underneath the fish and on the baking tray. Slice 2 orange and red (bell) peppers, toss with 2 tablespoons of olive oil, salt and pepper. Lay them around the fish to roast with it. They will get nice and charred. Serve with fresh parsley or coriander (cilantro), the orange slices and a good drizzle of olive oil.

SQUID INK PASTA
WITH CHILLI AND CRAB

Serves 2, 4 for sharing
Prep 5 minutes
Total 20 minutes

---

salt and freshly ground black pepper

400 g (1 lb) dried squid ink pasta

2 tablespoons olive oil, plus more for the pasta

1 jalapeño chilli, seeded and diced

2 garlic cloves, grated or minced

3 tablespoons white wine

400 g (14 oz) picked white lump crab meat

juice of 1 lemon

30 g (1¼ oz/1 cup) baby rocket (arugula)

2 tablespoons panko breadcrumbs

extra-virgin olive oil, for drizzling

✎ Substitute the crab for 10 peeled and deveined prawns (shrimp) (400 g/ 14 oz). After you add the garlic and chilli, add the prawns and cook until they are pink and no longer opaque, about 4 minutes total. Then mix in the pasta.

▦ Use leftover panko breadcrumbs in Baked chicken and ricotta meatballs (page 40).

When I was living in London, I would always bring my nephews, who were seven and five at the time, squid ink pasta (upon request) from Italy whenever I'd return from a trip, along with chocolates and other random gifts. I don't know if I was more excited that they loved squid ink pasta at that age or loved it as much as I do, so it will always have a special place in my heart. I do feel like this is one of those dishes that seems super fancy and is often found on restaurant menus, but it's really so quick and easy to put together at home.

⏱ Heat the water and use that waiting time to prep the chilli, and measure out the wine. If you have time, at the beginning of the recipe toast the breadcrumbs in a dry pan over a medium-heat until browned and crunchy. (The recipe will still be good if you don't!)

Method

1. Bring the water in a flameproof casserole dish (Dutch oven) to a vigorous boil and season with salt until it tastes like the sea (kind of like when you get a mouthful after getting knocked over by a wave. We've all been there). Add the pasta, breaking it in half if necessary (yes, many Italians would shun me for this) to make sure all pieces are submerged, and cook 4 minutes less than the package instructions, stirring every few minutes to make sure nothing is sticking to the bottom.

2. Drain the pasta into a colander in the sink, reserving 250 ml (1 cup) of the cooking water and immediately drizzle with olive oil, using the tongs to toss and coat the pasta, leaving it in the sink.

3. Wipe out the pot with a paper towel. Heat 2 tablespoons of the olive oil and the chilli over medium heat until shimmering and fragrant, about 1 minute. Add the garlic, stirring constantly until fragrant, about 30 seconds. Add the wine, cooking until the liquid reduces and pan looks almost dry, about 2 minutes. Mix in the pasta, reserved water, crab meat and lemon juice, stirring to combine until the pasta is warmed through, about 2 minutes. Season with salt. Remove the pan from the heat and stir in the rocket. Divide between bowls, finishing with breadcrumbs, pepper and extra-virgin olive oil.

LOOK MORE IMPRESSIVE THAN THEY ARE

A DIP INTO THE SEA

Serves 2, 4 for sharing
Prep 5 minutes
Total 25 minutes

---

2 tablespoons olive oil

1 shallot, thinly sliced

salt and freshly ground black pepper

2 teaspoons harissa, or more as desired

2 x 400 g (14 oz) tins chopped tomatoes
  and their liquid

250 ml (8½ fl oz/1 cup) water

225 g (½ lb) fillet flaky white fish, such
  as cod, halibut or flounder

450 g (½ lb) mussels, debearded and
  scrubbed (page 60)

225 g (½ lb) medium peeled prawns
  (shrimp), deveined

225 g (½ lb) scallops, muscles removed

15 g (½ oz/½ cup) fresh herbs like basil,
  parsley or coriander (cilantro), leaves
  and fine stems roughly chopped,
  for sprinkling

crusty bread, for serving

---

i Make sure you store your seafood
in a bowl over a bag of ice to maintain
its freshness and keep it at an optimal
temperature. Ask your fishmonger or
supermarket for a bag of ice. Seafood
such as clams and mussels are alive and
need air to breathe, so keep the bags
that they are in open. After cooking,
discard any that don't open as they
were most likely not alive when you
started cooking.

This recipe is kind of a cioppino, sort of a bouillabaisse, and also not either of those things. It is a pot of spiced tomato sauce filled with fresh seafood, that we know for sure. Harissa adds a bit of a kick and depth to the tomato sauce, which is great for us as this can cook quickly and be on the table to wow your friend, partner or dinner guests. It's a fabulous one to do to impress people as it looks kinda fancy. Don't forget to serve it with thick, crusty bread, preferably drizzled with some olive oil then lightly toasted.

Method

1. Heat the oil in a large flameproof casserole dish (Dutch oven) over a medium heat until shimmering. Add the shallot and a pinch of salt, stirring occasionally until softened, about 3 minutes. Stir in the harissa and cook together until the spices start tickling your nose, about 30 seconds.

2. Pour in the tomatoes and water, raising the heat to bring the liquid to an active boil then reduce to maintain an active simmer. Cook until the tomatoes naturally break down into smaller pieces and sauce thickens, about 10–12 minutes. Taste and adjust the seasoning with salt and pepper.

3. Add the white fish (it will naturally flake and break apart into smaller pieces during the cooking process) and mussels, stirring to coat with the sauce. Cover and cook for 2 minutes, then mix in the prawns and scallops. Keep covered until most of the mussel shells have opened and the prawns are pink and no longer translucent, about 3 minutes more. Discard any shells that have not opened. While the seafood is cooking, chop the herbs and toast the bread. Definitely pour some wine.

4. Ladle into bowls. Place an empty bowl for the shells on the table, top with herbs and serve with the bread.

GINGER-CURRIED LAMB CHOPS WITH BRAISED GREENS

Serves 2, 4 for sharing
Prep 5 minutes
Total 20 minutes

2 tablespoons curry powder

1 teaspoon ground ginger (optional)

salt and freshly ground black pepper

4 lamb chops

1½ tablespoons ghee or vegetable oil

1 medium red onion, thinly sliced

2 garlic cloves, grated or minced

120 ml (4 fl oz/½ cup) low-salt chicken stock (broth)

100 g (3½ oz/2 packed cups) chard or other leafy greens, leaves removed from the stems, leaves and tender stems cut into 5 cm (2 in) pieces

juice of 1 lemon

15 g (½ oz/½ cup) fresh mint, parsley or coriander (cilantro) leaves and fine stems, roughly chopped, for sprinkling

extra-virgin olive oil, for drizzling

✏ French-trimmed chops means the bone is cleaned off for a more attractive presentation; however, for our purposes, I prefer not to do that as the rendered fat from the bone area seasons the braised greens. But either will work.

When living in London, I made it my mission to try every Indian restaurant I could find to figure out my favourite, from visiting suburban haunts to Michelin-starred restaurants.

I hit more than worth discussing, but I did visit the main contenders: Tayyabs, Gymkhana, Trishna, Dishoom and Gunpowder. What really won my heart over were the tandoori lamb chops at sister restaurants Trishna and Gymkhana. The rich, intense spices, crunchy crust and soft, tender meat had me making a visit every few months and bringing friends and family to share in the joy. Though all of the offerings make London such a wonderful city to explore Indian cuisine in. This is my tribute to both fantastic lamb chops and eating adventures.

Method

1. In a mixing bowl, combine the curry powder, ginger, salt and pepper. Season the chops all over with the spice mix and set aside while you prep the rest of the ingredients.

2. Heat the ghee in a 30 cm (12 in) frying pan (skillet) over a medium-high heat until melted. Add the chops and cook without moving until the bottom layer is kind of bubbling and browning, about 3–4 minutes, then flip and continue to cook until the internal temperature reaches 55°C (130°F) on an instant-read thermometer, about 3–4 minutes longer for medium rare. Remove from the frying pan and set aside on a cutting board to rest, covering loosely with foil.

3. Return the frying pan to a medium heat without wiping it out. (There should still be about 1 tablespoon of fat in the pan, add more if needed.) Add the onion and a pinch of salt and cook until just softened, about 2–3 minutes, then add the garlic, stirring constantly until fragrant, about 30 seconds. Pour in the stock, scraping up any brown bits with a wooden spoon. Immediately add the greens, stirring occasionally, until softened and most of the liquid is gone, about 3–4 minutes. Season to taste with salt and pepper. Off heat, stir in the lemon juice.

4. Divide the greens and lamb chops on serving plates, sprinkle with fresh herbs, drizzle with olive oil, and serve immediately.

GARLICKY CLAMS
WITH FRESH HERBS AND WHITE WINE

Serves 2, 4 for sharing
Prep 5 minutes
Total 15 minutes

2 tablespoons olive oil

1 teaspoon dried red chilli flakes

3 garlic cloves, grated or minced

salt and freshly ground black pepper

250 ml (8½ fl oz/1 cup) white wine

1.3 kg (3 lb/about 24–30 clams) small clams, preferably Littlenecks, scrubbed

crusty bread, for serving

15 g (½ oz/½ cup) fresh parsley, basil or coriander (cilantro) leaves and fine stems, roughly chopped

juice of 1 lemon

When storing clams, keep them in an open bag over ice in a bowl.

In the later summer months when tomatoes are in season, add 300 g (10½ oz/2 cups) halved Sungold or cherry tomatoes to the recipe with the clams. If you don't want to halve them, prick them with a fork tine so they easily break apart. Let them cook and burst open.

Cook a pot of pasta, run it through generously with olive oil, let drain in the sink and add to the pan when the clams are done with 60–120 ml (¼–½ cup) reserved pasta water, if dry, then stir and serve.

When visiting the North Fork of Long Island in New York with a few friends, we decided to make this dish after a picture-perfect day filled with beaches, farm stands and fish markets. Back at our rental home, we realised that the only salt we had were whole, Himalayan rock crystals with no way to grind them.

'We'll just crush them like you do peppercorns', was my answer, meaning to wrap said peppercorns in a dish towel then smash them with a pan (page 16). This didn't work on tough salt crystals. We made very little progress.

'Let's run it over with the car!' was the next suggestion.

I placed the dish towel on the ground, and my friend drove back and forth across it. Needless to say, it did not work.

As another friend later said, 'how could two smart people do such a dumb thing?' It is impossible for me to think of this dish and not laugh about the time we tried to crush salt by driving it over with a car.

Method

1. Heat the oil and chilli flakes in a 30 cm (12 in) frying pan (skillet) with a tight-fitting lid or casserole dish (Dutch oven) over a medium heat until shimmering. Add the garlic and salt, cooking until fragrant but not browned, about 30 seconds. Add the white wine, use a wooden spoon to loosen anything caught on the bottom of the pan and raise the heat to medium-high, then adjust to bring it to an active simmer (avoid boiling). You should start smelling the wine notes wafting up.

2. Add the clams, cover and adjust the heat to maintain an active simmer until most of them open, about 6–8 minutes (larger clams might take a bit longer). Discard any that don't. Use this time to toast the bread, set the table and pour the wine, as you'll want to eat right when they are done.

3. Off the heat, stir in the parsley and lemon juice, seasoning to taste with salt and pepper. Divide between bowls and serve with bread.

LOOK MORE IMPRESSIVE THAN THEY ARE

SKIRT STEAK TACOS

WITH CHARRED CORN AND SPICY MAYO

Serves 4
Prep 15 minutes
Total 30 minutes

---

1 tablespoon ground cumin

½ teaspoon ground cayenne pepper

salt and freshly ground black pepper

550–675 g (1¼–½ lb) skirt steak, trimmed and cut crosswise into 12 cm (5 in) pieces

1½ tablespoons ghee or 50 ml (1¾ fl oz/¼ cup) rapeseed (canola) oil

2 sweetcorn cobs, kernels removed (about 1½ cups) (page 166)

½ medium red onion, diced

1 jalapeño chilli, seeded and diced

2 spring onions (scallions), white and light green parts only, thinly sliced

1 tablespoon Sriracha sauce or more, if desired

50 g (1¾ oz/¼ cup) Kewpie (see headnote) or regular mayonnaise

4 limes, juice of 2, 2 cut into wedges, for serving

15 g (½ oz/½ cup) fresh coriander (cilantro) leaves and fine stems, roughly chopped

1 ripe Hass avocado, halved, destoned, peeled and sliced

corn or flour tortillas, toasted in a dry frying pan (skillet) or in the oven and kept warm in foil (page 166)

Pickled red onions, to serve (page 54)

✏ 170 g (6 oz) steak per person will yield about 2–3 tacos per person.

Mayonnaise was a touchy subject for me growing up, mostly because my sister went through a brief period being obsessed with it. She would eat 'mayo and turkey sandwiches' with a thin slice of turkey and globs of mayo. Like a haunting nightmare, I can still picture her picking up the pieces of bread and that gentle pressure causing thick, white mayo to ooze out, sliding down the crusts and onto her hands.

But that all changed when I tried this sriracha mayo combo. I prefer using Kewpie mayo, a Japanese mayonnaise that's made with rice vinegar and egg yolks instead of distilled vinegar and whole eggs, because I like the taste better, but, let's be serious, it's probably a little bit because of my childhood as well. You can try your way with both.

⏱ First coat the steak in the spice mixture. Then prep the corn, onions, chilli and spring onions (scallions). You can do the rest as it all cooks.

Method

1. Stir together the cumin, cayenne, salt and pepper in a shallow mixing bowl. Rub the steak with the mixture, getting into all the cracks and crevices, and set aside at room temperature. Your kitchen will likely get smoky, so turn on the extractor fan, open some windows or do what you need to do.

2. In a 30 cm (12 in) cast iron pan, heat the ghee or oil over a medium-high heat until melted or lightly smoking. Add the steak in an even layer and cook without touching until a dark crust has formed on the bottom, about 3 minutes, then use tongs to turn over and cook until the other side is also browned (another 2–3 minutes for medium rare), or until an instant-read thermometer registers 52°C (125°F), depending on thickness of steak, or 58°C (135°F) for medium. If the steaks char too quickly, then flip them continuously until done. Transfer them to a large plate, cover loosely with foil, and let rest.

Continued on the next page

To warm tortillas: Heat in a 90°C (200°F) oven on a baking tray (sheet pan) or toast in a dry frying pan (skillet). Wrap in foil to stay warm.

How to remove corn from the cob: In a mixing bowl (preferably one that you will use that day), use a paring knife to shave off the kernels so that they get caught in the bowl rather than scatter all over the kitchen.

3. Meanwhile, pour off all but 1 tablespoon of fat from the pan and reduce to a medium heat. Add the corn, onion, jalapeño, the white part of the spring onions and season with salt. Cook until the corn begins to char, and the onions and jalapeño softens, about 5–6 minutes.

4. While that's cooking, mix the Sriracha and mayo in a small bowl until combined, adjusting the heat preference to taste. Sprinkle the avocado with salt and juice of ½ lime. Set on a cutting board.

5. Scrape the corn mixture into a large bowl and add the juice of 1 lime or more to taste, coriander and the remaining green parts of the spring onion and stir to combine. Season with salt and pepper. Slice the steak across the grain and serve with corn salsa, spicy mayo, lime wedges, the pickled red onions and avocado slices. Let everyone DIY their own tacos.

Photo overleaf

Once when I was in New Orleans, we had a 45-minute wait for brunch and wandered over to a nearby restaurant to get a drink, as one does, and it had a make-your-own bloody Mary bar (!!!). I still feel like this was a highlight of my life. There were rows of toppings, from pickled dilly beans, celery stalks, spiced and skewered prawns (shrimp), olives, cornichons and so on. It was incredible, as I'm always a fan of when you can eat and drink at the same time.

Ever since, I've realised the joy that lays in DIY bars of any sort, and this extends to taco parties. Proteins like steak, prawns, chicken and then tons of toppings that all go together. Be this charred corn salad, a *pico de gallo* of sorts, guacamole, fresh herbs and so on. Put some hot sauce or perhaps Sriracha mayo on the side and let people do their thing. It takes the pressure off you as a host and is fun for everyone.

Plus, tacos are some of the greatest foods of all time. I prefer corn tortillas, but you can do flour or offer a choice of both on the table, just keep them warm in foil. With that said, none of these are traditional tacos, but more ones that are easy, full of bold flavours and ones you can totally make look more impressive than they really are.

Set these up on a table so everyone can DIY their own tacos.

TACOS FOR A PARTY

Prawns (shrimp)
Season 450 g (1 lb) peeled and deveined prawns with salt, pepper, 1 teaspoon of cayenne pepper and cook in 2 tablespoons of oil over medium-high heat until pink and no longer opaque, about 2 minutes per side. Finish with the juice of 2 limes.

Chicken
Buy half a rotisserie chicken (about 450 g/1 lb), shred with your fingers, heat 2 tablespoons of olive oil over a medium heat until shimmering, add 1–2 chopped chipotle chillies in adobo (depending on your heat preference) and 1–2 teaspoons of its sauce, until fragrant, about 1 minute. Add the chicken, tossing to combine and cook until warmed through, about 2 minutes. Finish with 2 tablespoons of lime juice. Serve with fresh coriander (cilantro), spicy mayo or other bar toppings.

Veg black beans
Heat 2 tablespoons of olive oil over a medium heat until shimmering. Add 1 red and yellow (bell) pepper, diced, ½ red onion, diced, 1 tin black beans (drained and rinsed), salt, pepper, 1 teaspoon of dried oregano and a pinch of cayenne pepper stirring frequently until softened, about 5 minutes. Definitely top this with avocado or mix some in the serving bowl and finish with coriander, spicy mayo or other bar toppings.

Guacamole
Combine 2 ripe Hass avocados, halved, stoned, peeled and cubed, ½ tablespoon of ground cumin (optional or adjust to taste), 1 jalapeño chilli, seeded and diced, 15 g (½ oz/½ cup) of fresh coriander leaves and fine stems, 2 spring onions (scallions), light white and green parts sliced, the juice of 2 limes or more, as needed, and salt to taste. If you're feeling lazy, slice up the avocado, sprinkle with salt and lime juice and serve for toppings at the bar.

Pico de gallo
Combine 1 garlic clove, grated or minced, 1 small diced red onion, 150 g (5 oz/1 cup) diced tomatoes, juice from 2 limes, or more to taste, 15 g (½ oz/½ cup) fresh coriander, leaves and fine stems roughly chopped and salt in a bowl and mix together. Adjust the seasoning to taste. This gets better as it sits so make it first.

THANK YOU!!!

To the behind-the-scenes team who brought this book to life, I couldn't have dreamed up a better group of talented, funny and inspiring women to work with. Molly Ahuja, it is a true gift to work with such a trusted friend and brilliant editor. Nicole Herft, Patricia Niven, Eila Purvis, Michelle Noel, Rosie Mackean and Mimi Aversa, thank you all for your infectious laughter, thoughtful suggestions and for being all-around good humans. You made this book infinitely better by being a part of it. And thank you to the Hardie Grant team for making this all possible.

Kenji López-Alt, Ed Levine and Serious Eats, thank you for your guidance, for giving me a shot and for letting me use some of my favourite Serious Eats recipes in this book.

To my lovely parents, thank you for making sure we gathered around the dinner table every night growing up; food will always be an expression of love for me because of this. To my darling sister, words can't express how much you've helped me in this lifetime – thank you for your input and recipe testing. Huge hugs to my recipe testers and personal cheerleaders, Diana, Matty, Maryse, Amanda and Lauren, and a huge thank you to my other dinner companions and tasters along the way for your valuable insights.

Thank you to all of the incredible people in my life whose names I can't list because I'm over my word count (sorry, Mols!). Please know that your support, encouragement and humour make me feel like such a lucky person to have you all in my life.

ABOUT THE AUTHOR

Yasmin Fahr is a food writer who loves eating out as much as she loves cooking at home. She has a penchant for cheesy phrases, lemons, feta and cumin (as you'll soon see). She went to Cornell University and then New York University for a master's in Food Studies. Her writing and recipes have appeared on The Kitchn, Epicurious, TASTE, *Bon Appetit*, Serious Eats, *Food & Wine* and others. She currently lives in New York with previous stints in London and Los Angeles.

INDEX

Keeping it Simple

Published in 2020 by Hardie Grant Books,
an imprint of Hardie Grant Publishing

Hardie Grant Books (London)
5th & 6th Floors
52–54 Southwark Street
London SE1 1UN

Hardie Grant Books (Melbourne)
Building 1, 658 Church Street
Richmond, Victoria 3121

hardiegrantbooks.com

Recipes on pages 77, 90, 107, 124, 132, 140, 152 and 165 are adapted from Serious Eats

British Library Cataloguing-in-Publication Data. A catalogue record for this book is available
from the British Library.

ISBN: 978-1-78488-282-2
10 9 8 7 6 5 4 3 2 1

Publishing Director: Kate Pollard
Senior Editor: Molly Ahuja
Junior Editor: Eila Purvis
Internal and Cover Design: Studio Noel
Internal Illustrations: Studio Noel
Photographer: Patricia Niven
Food Stylist: Nicole Herft
Copy Editor: Eve Marleau
Proofreader: Jane Bamforth
Indexer: Cathy Heath

Colour Reproduction by p2d
Printed and bound in China by Leo Paper Productions Ltd.